Teach Yourself To Play Guitar

MORTY MANUS & RON MANUS

Acoustic guitar cover photo courtesy of Martin Guitar Company.
Fender Stratocaster® photograph by J. Jeff Leland.
Fender Stratocaster® courtesy of Carl Culpepper.

Cover Design: Ted Engelbart
Book Design: Susan Hartman
Production: Bruce Merrill Goldes / Paul Woodring

Alfred
Alfred Publishing Co., Inc.
16320 Roscoe Blvd., Suite 100
P.O. Box 10003
Van Nuys, CA 91410-0003
alfred.com

ISBN-10: 0-88284-675-2 (Book)   ISBN-10: 0-88284-679-5 (Book and CD)
ISBN-13: 978-0-88284-675-0 (Book)   ISBN-13: 978-0-88284-679-8 (Book and CD)

GETTING STARTED — A SHORT HISTORY OF THE GUITAR

Instruments related to the guitar have been in existence since ancient times. The idea of stretching strings across a vibrating chamber of air, called a sound box, dates back to prehistoric times, and is found in virtually every culture in the world. The idea of using frets to mark the tones in a scale probably comes from India where to this day players of the vina and sitar tie pieces of catgut across the fingerboards of their instruments to act as frets. Early explorers from Spain and Portugal probably brought the idea to Europe and, of course, the European settlers brought guitars with them to America.

Guitars closely resembling today's classical guitars (see page 3) were well-known during the 19th century. They were particularly popular among the less well-to-do and mobile members of society because of their low cost and easy portability.

Early jazz bands and dance orchestras tended to favor the banjo as a chordal instrument because of its more penetrating tone. Then, in the late 1920s, new advances in electronics made the electric guitar feasible for the first time. The guitar's sound could then be amplified and could compete with the loudest brass or woodwind instruments. By the late 1930s, the banjo was all but forgotten and the electric guitar was common in jazz groups and dance orchestras.

The next innovation came in the late '40s. Engineers realized that the hollow wood body of the guitar was no longer necessary as a generator of a musical signal, so the sound box was eliminated and the result was the solid body electric guitar. Since then there have been many modifications in the design of guitars, but basically they all are either acoustic—producing a sound by vibrating a string over a sound box—or electric—producing a sound by vibrating a string and amplifying and modifying that sound electronically. Using this book you can teach yourself how to play the guitar if you have either type.

GETTING STARTED TYPES OF GUITARS

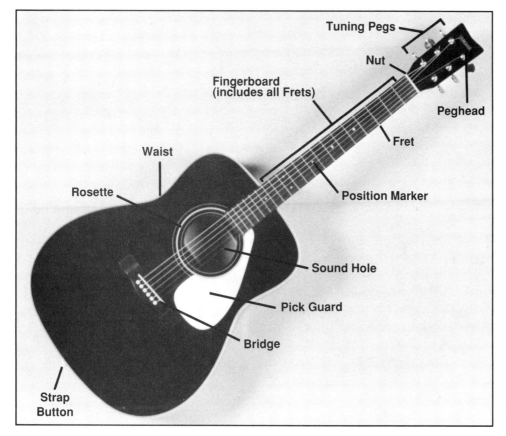

Acoustic Flat Top Guitar

Acoustic Flat Top guitars have narrow necks and steel strings. They are either strummed with a flat pick or played with one or more finger picks. They are used in rock, blues, country and folk playing.

Strings: Steel
Gauge: Light or Medium

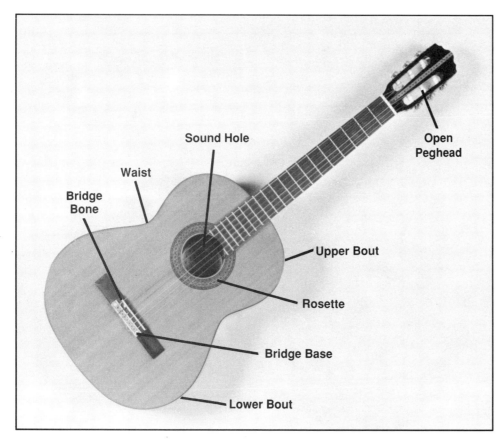

Classical Guitar

Classical guitars have flat tops, wide necks, and nylon strings. They are always played with the fingers.

Strings: Nylon
Gauge: Varied

TYPES OF GUITARS

Solid Body Electric Guitar

Solid body electrics have narrow necks, light-gauge strings and one or more electrical pickups. The output of these pickups is fed through an amplifier and is sometimes modified further by using wah-wah pedals, distortion pedals, choruses or other means of altering the tone. Solid body electrics are used almost exclusively for rock, heavy metal, blues, country and jazz music.

Strings: Steel
Gauge: Light

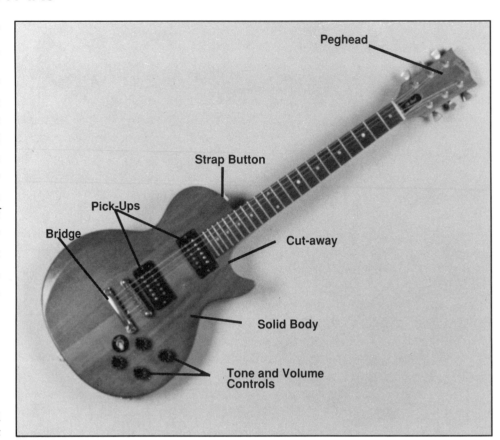

Thin Body Electric Guitar

Thin body electrics are semi-hollow guitars with electrical pickups. This gives the guitar a warm, rich sound. They are good for jazz, blues, rock and fusion.

Strings: Steel
Gauge: Medium

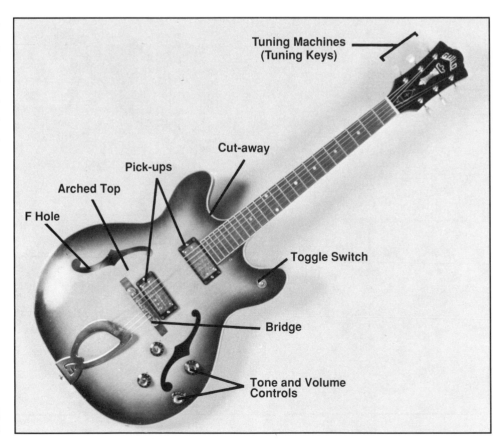

Buying A Guitar

First, ask yourself what kind of music you like the most. Then choose the model from pages 3 and 4 that is recommended for that style. If you wish to play classical music only, you should not be playing from this book, which is intended for players interested in rock, heavy metal, blues, country, jazz, folk and other popular styles.

New or Used?

Often a used guitar can be a very good investment as well as a satisfying instrument to play. However, it is important not to attempt to buy a used guitar without the advice of someone who is very knowledgeable about the instrument and whom you trust. If you buy a new guitar, make sure you purchase it at a reliable music store. It is important to choose a place that has been in business a long time and that has the capability to service your instrument.

What Kind of Strings?

Guides that recommend which kind of strings to use are indicated below the photos of the guitars on pages 3 and 4. Nylon and silk-and-steel strings are easy on the fingers of a beginner. Steel strings are harder to push down but project a more brilliant sound. If you decide to start with steel strings ask for "light gauge." If you desire you can work your way up to medium or heavy gauge as your fingers grow stronger and tougher.

Caring for Your Guitar

Most guitar care is simply common sense. Rule one is never to expose the instrument to extremes of heat or cold. This means if your take your guitar outside, keep it out of the sun. It also means that you don't leave it in the unheated trunk of a car in the winter. Rule two is to make sure the strings are tuned to an accurate pitch. Tuning the strings too high can have serious consequences for the instrument, causing the neck to bow or the bridge to rip out of the top. Other things you can do are to wipe the strings off after playing and to polish the instrument using guitar polish, which you can get at any music store. It won't hurt to ask your repairman to check over the instrument twice a year—just before the summer and winter.

TUNING YOUR GUITAR Track 1

First make sure the strings are wound properly around the tuning pegs. They should go from inside to outside. See below:

4th or D String

5th or A String

6th or E String

Turning the tuning key counter-clockwise (always from the point of view of the player) raises the pitch. Turning the tuning key clockwise lowers the pitch.

Some guitars have the six tuning pegs on the same side of the head. Make sure all six strings are wound the same way, from inside out.

3rd or G String

2nd or B String

1st or E String

Once your strings are stretched across the guitar properly, listen to the Teach Yourself recording for this book, and follow the directions to get the guitar in perfect tune.

If you do not have the Teach Yourself recording, follow these directions to get the instrument in tune.

Important: Always remember that the thinnest, highest string—the one closest to the floor—is the first string. The thickest, lowest string—the one closest to the ceiling—is the sixth string. When guitarists say "the highest string," they mean the one highest in pitch, not the one highest in position.

How to Tune Your Guitar Without Using a Cassette or CD

The six strings of your guitar have the same pitches as the six notes shown on the piano in the following illustration:

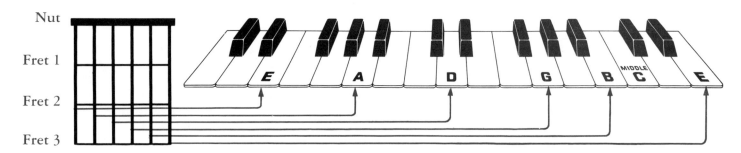

Tune the sixth string to E on the piano. If no piano is available and you do not have the Teach Yourself recording, we recommend you buy a tuning fork, tuning pipe or electric tuner. The first two are inexpensive and very handy, and all three are available from your music dealer.

Press 5th fret of 6th string to get pitch of 5th string (A).

Press 5th fret of 5th string to get pitch of 4th string (D).

Press 5th fret of 4th string to get pitch of 3rd string (G).

Press 4th fret of 3rd string to get pitch of 2nd string (B).

Press 5th fret of 2nd string to get pitch of 1st string (E).

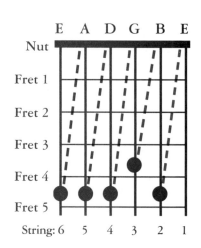

HOLDING THE GUITAR

▲ *Sitting*

▲ *Sitting with left leg crossed over right*

▲ *Sitting with right leg crossed over left*

▲ *Standing, with strap*

▲ *Standing with foot on stool*

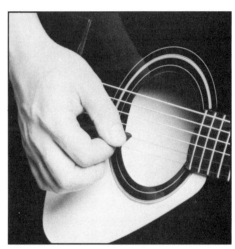

▲ *Holding the pick*

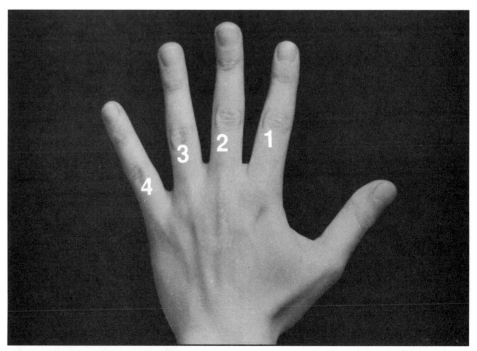

▲ *Numbering the left-hand fingers*

 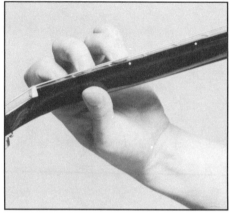

HOLDING THE GUITAR (cont'd.)

The Left-Hand Position

Note that the thumb falls about opposite the joint of the second and third fingers. Keep the elbow in and the fingers curved.

▲ *The left hand position from the front*   ▲ *The left hand position from the back*

 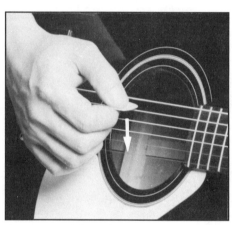

The Right-Hand Position

The pick is held firmly, but without squeezing it hard enough to cause tension in the right arm. The motion is a relaxed downward sweep of the wrist, not the entire arm.

▲ *Position of the right arm*   ▲ *Motion of the pick*

Placing the Finger on a String

When you place a left-hand finger on a string, make sure you press firmly and as close to the fret wire as you can without actually being right on it. This will ensure a clean, bright tone.

▲ *THIS*
Finger presses the string down near the fret without actually being on it.

▲ *NOT THIS*
Finger is too far from fret wire; tone is "buzzy" and indefinite.

▲ *NOT THIS*
Finger is on top of fret wire; tone is muffled and unclear.

GETTING ACQUAINTED WITH MUSIC

Notes

Musical sounds are indicated by symbols called NOTES. Their time value is determined by their color (white or black) and by stems and flags attached to the note.

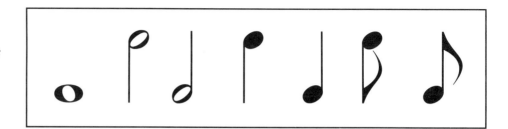

The Staff

The name and pitch of the notes are determined by the note's position on a graph made of five horizontal lines, and the spaces in between, called the staff. The notes are named after the first seven letters of the alphabet (A–G), repeated to embrace the entire range of musical sound.

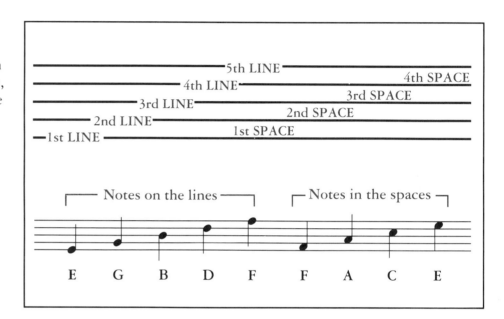

Measures and Bar Lines

Music is also divided into equal parts, called MEASURES. One measure is divided from another by a BAR LINE.

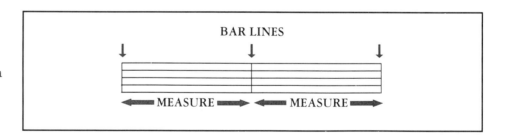

Clefs

During the evolution of music notation, the staff had from two to twenty lines, and symbols were invented to locate a reference line, or pitch, by which all other pitches were determined. These symbols were called clefs.

Music for the guitar is written in the G or treble clef. Originally the Gothic letter G was used on a four-line staff to establish the pitch of G:

GETTING ACQUAINTED WITH TABLATURE

GETTING STARTED

Tablature is a graphic method of showing how to play notes and chords on the guitar. It uses a six-line staff, each line representing one string of the guitar.

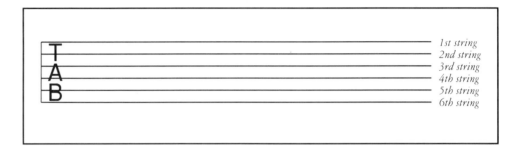

A number placed on a line means to play that fret on the corresponding string. Thus,

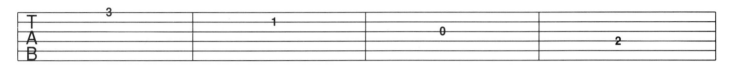

Play the 1st string, 3rd fret   2nd string, 1st fret   3rd string, open   4th string, 2nd fret

Numbers placed one on top of the other are played simultaneously.

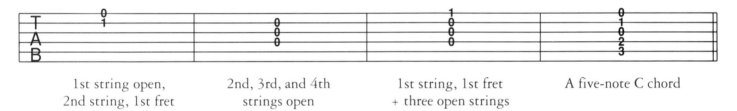

1st string open,   2nd, 3rd, and 4th   1st string, 1st fret   A five-note C chord
2nd string, 1st fret   strings open   + three open strings

CHORD DIAGRAMS

Chord diagrams are used to indicate fingering for chords. The example to the right means to place your first finger on the first fret, second string and second finger on the second fret, fourth string. Then strum the first four strings only. The x's on the fifth and sixth strings indicate not to play these.

To make it as clear as possible, all the material in this book appears both in traditional music and in tablature. Chord diagrams are included where appropriate.

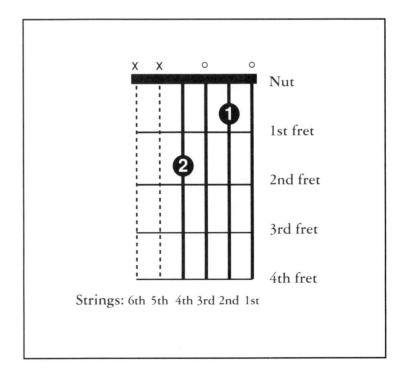

Strings: 6th 5th 4th 3rd 2nd 1st

Notes on the First String E

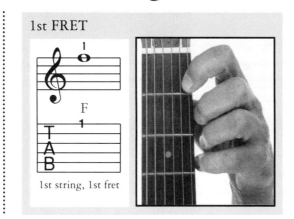

Playing the first string open (the note E):

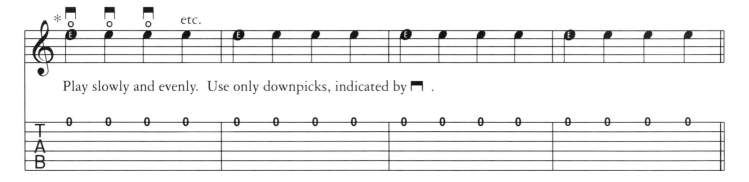

Play slowly and evenly. Use only downpicks, indicated by ◻ .

Combining the fingered notes F and G with the open string E:

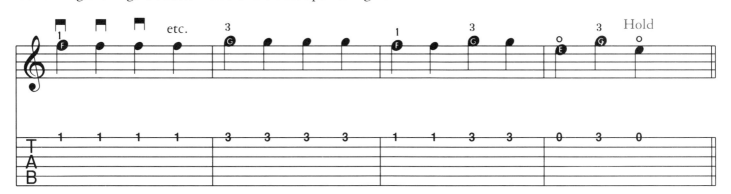

Measures and Bar Lines
Music is also divided into equal parts, called MEASURES. One measure is divided from another by a BAR LINE.

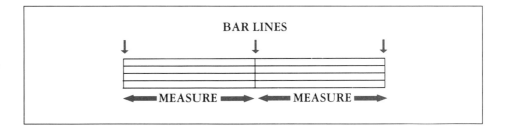

*○ means OPEN STRING

Mixing It Up Track 3

Left-hand fingers: When playing from the first to the third fret, keep the first finger down. Only the G will sound, but when you go back to the F, your finger will already be in place, making the transition sound smoother.

Keep 1st finger down _____

Go to next line without stopping

Keep 1st finger down _____

A double bar line marks the end of a piece.

More Mixing Track 4

Left-hand fingers: Place as close to the fret wires as possible without actually touching them.

Keep 1st finger down __ ┘   Keep 1st finger down _____

Keep 1st finger down _____

SOUND OFF: HOW TO COUNT TIME

(MINI MUSIC LESSON)

4 Kinds of Notes:

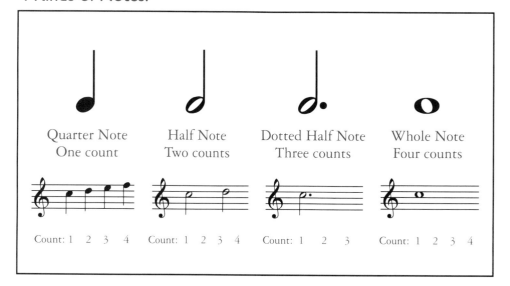

Time Signatures

Each piece of music has two numbers at its beginning called a time signature. These numbers tell us how to count time for that particular piece.

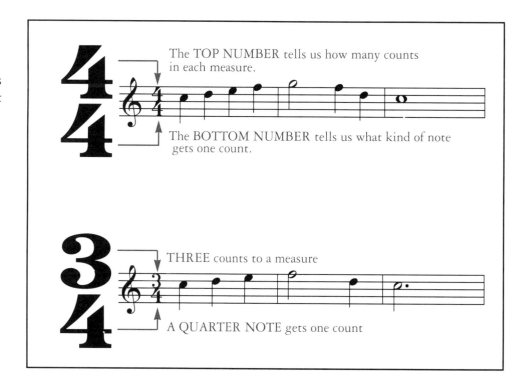

Important:

Fill in the missing time signatures of the songs already learned. Even though tablature players do not read standard music notation, it is still important to become familiar with the concept of time signatures.

PLAYING DIFFERENT KINDS OF NOTES AND TIME SIGNATURES Track 5

Half Notes (two counts)

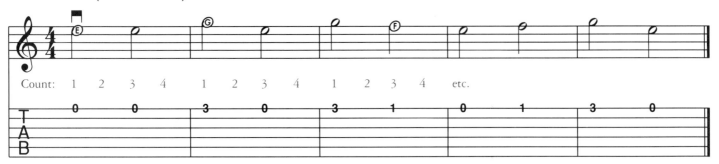

Dotted Half Notes (three counts)

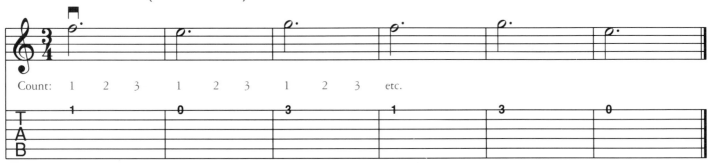

Whole Notes (four counts)

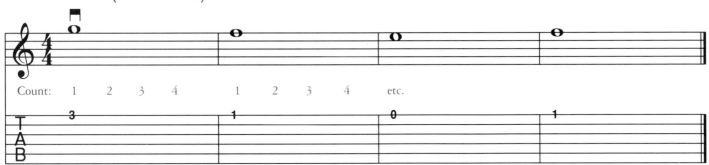

Mixed Notes (review)

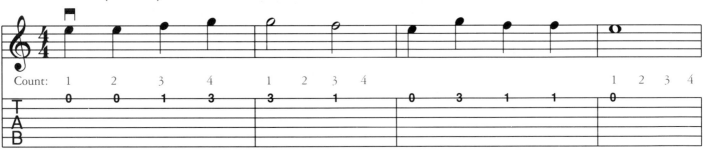

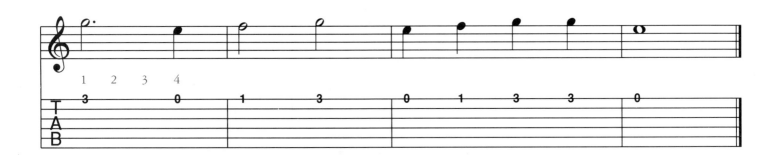

Notes on the Second String B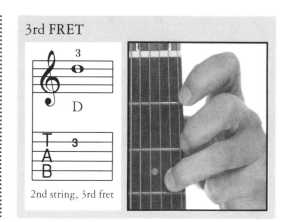

OPEN STRING	1st FRET		3rd FRET	

 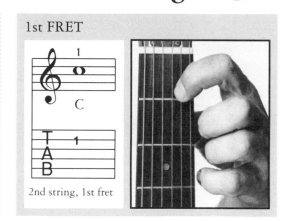

2nd string, open   2nd string, 1st fret   2nd string, 3rd fret

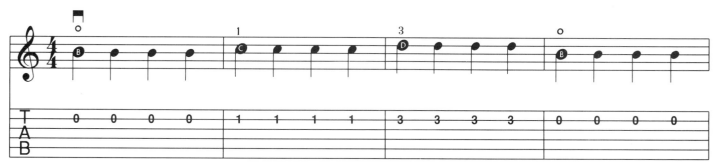

Two-String Rock

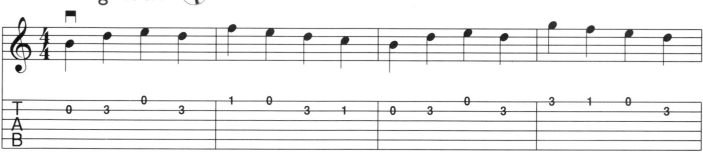

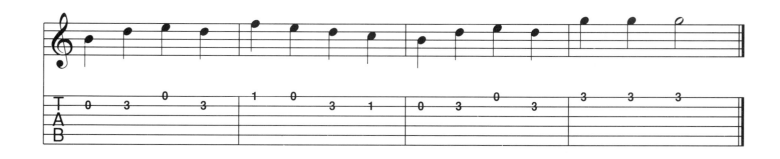

Beautiful Brown Eyes Track 8

Guitar Rock Track 9

Merry-Go-Round Track 10

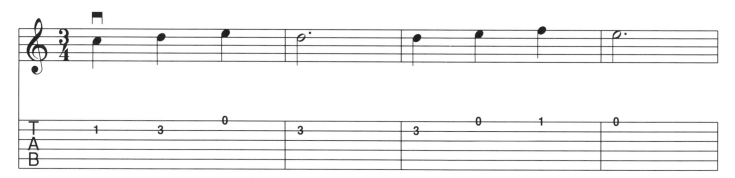

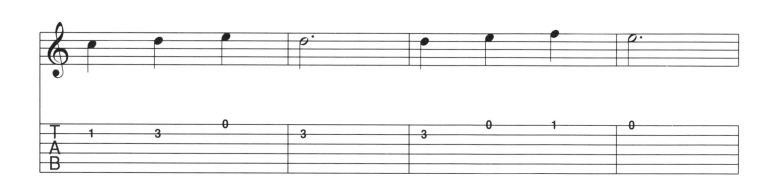

Jingle Bells

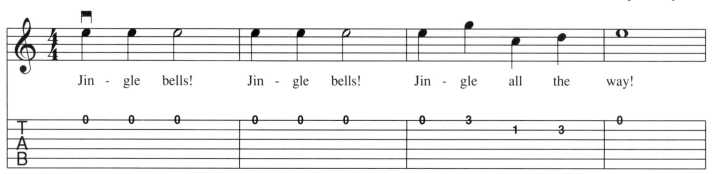

Track 11

J. Pierpont

Jin - gle bells!   Jin - gle bells!   Jin - gle   all   the   way!

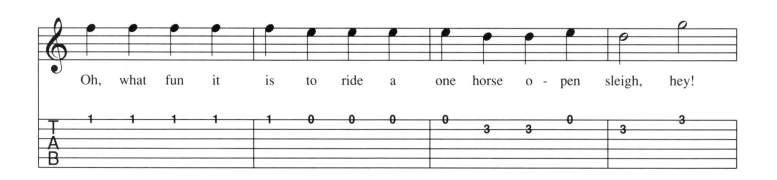

Oh,   what   fun   it   is   to   ride   a   one   horse   o - pen   sleigh,   hey!

Jin - gle   bells!   Jin - gle   bells!   Jin - gle   all   the   way!

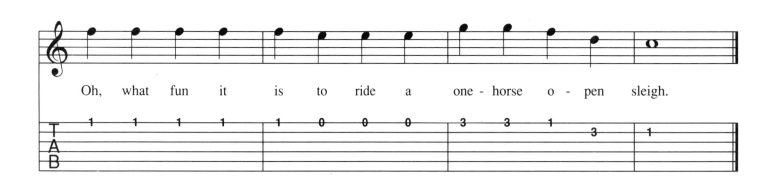

Oh,   what   fun   it   is   to   ride   a   one - horse   o - pen   sleigh.

Notes on the Third String G

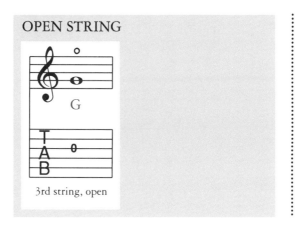

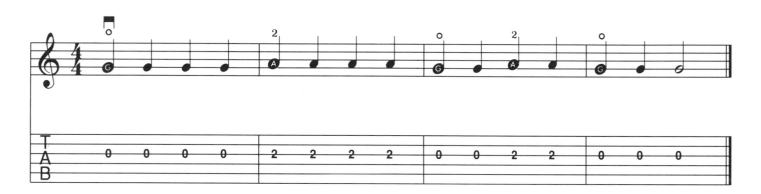

Au Clair de la Lune

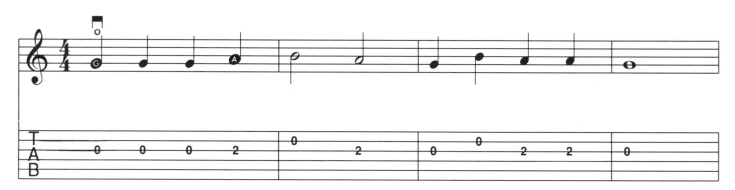

Three-String Rock   Track 14

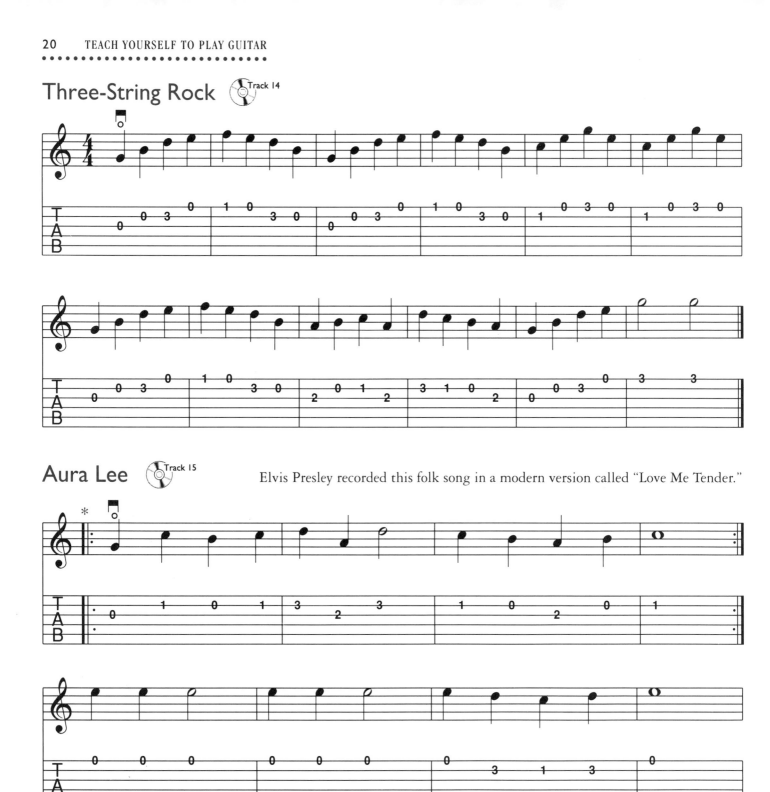

Aura Lee   Track 15

Elvis Presley recorded this folk song in a modern version called "Love Me Tender."

*The double dots on the inside of the double bars indicate that everything between the double bars must be REPEATED.

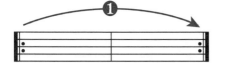

Largo from the New World Symphony

Use down-strokes only until further notice.

Dvořák

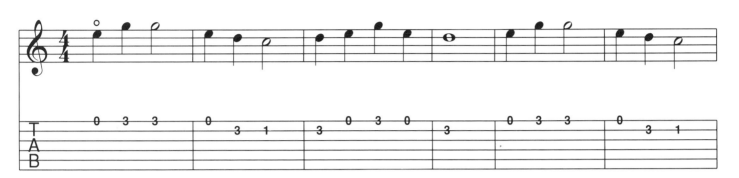

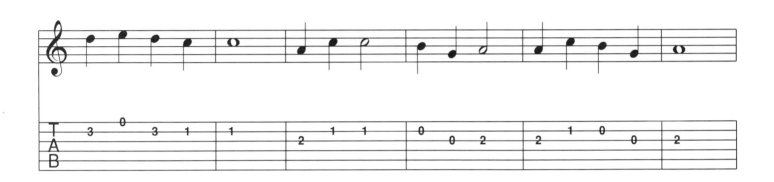

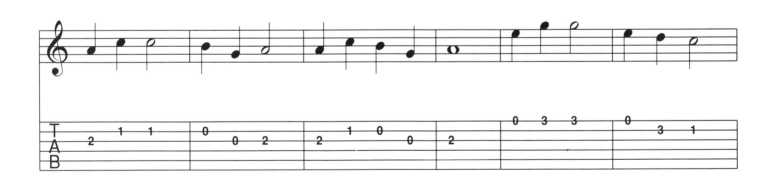

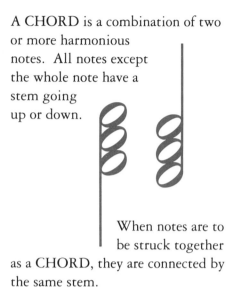

INTRODUCING CHORDS Track 17

A CHORD is a combination of two or more harmonious notes. All notes except the whole note have a stem going up or down.

When notes are to be struck together as a CHORD, they are connected by the same stem.

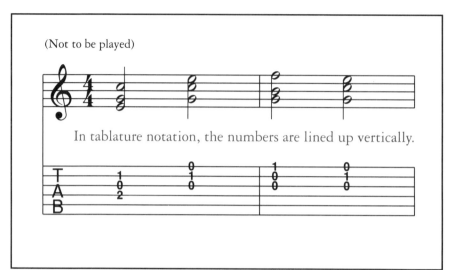

(Not to be played)

In tablature notation, the numbers are lined up vertically.

Meet the Chords

Two-note chords on the open B and E strings.

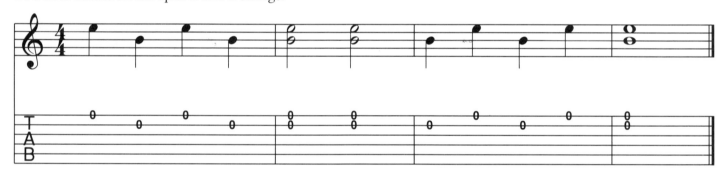

Two-note chords on the open G and B strings.

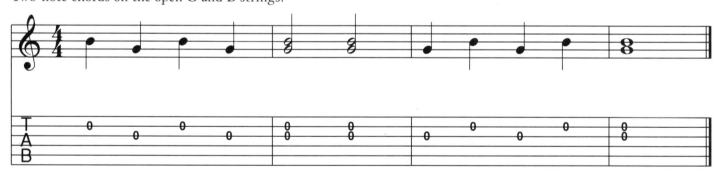

Three-note chords on the open G, B and E strings.

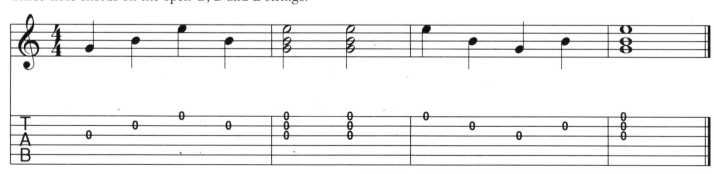

The Three-String C Chord

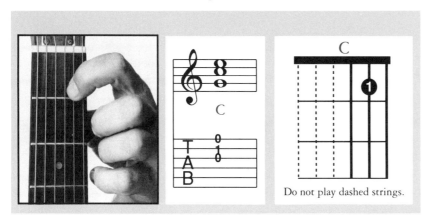

Do not play dashed strings.

The chords you played on page 22 use only combinations of open strings. The next chord is called the C chord. It uses one finger plus the 1st and 3rd open strings.

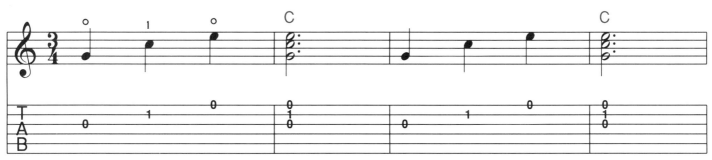

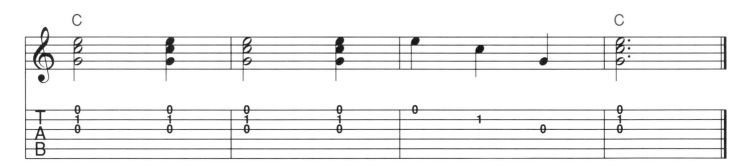

Ode To Joy (theme from the 9th symphony)

Beethoven

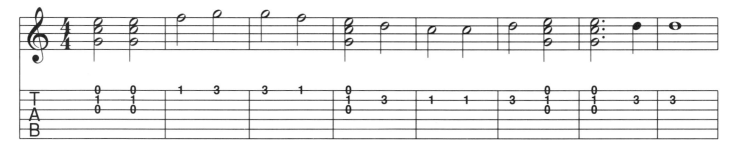

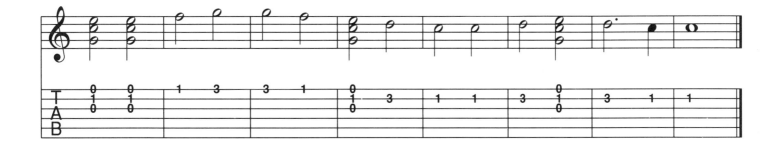

INTRODUCING THE QUARTER REST

 Track 20

This strange-looking rest is used in music notation to mean one beat of silence. First play the exercise, then try the rock song.

For a cleaner effect when an open-string note is followed by a rest, you may stop the sound of the strings by touching them lightly with the "heel" of the right hand.

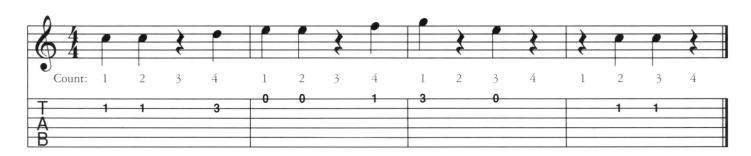

Rock 'n' Rhythm 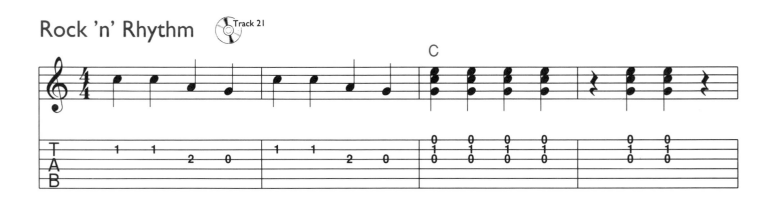 Track 21

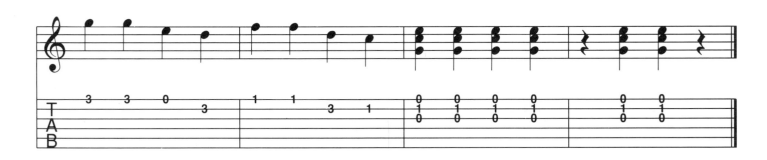

The Three-String G⁷ Chord 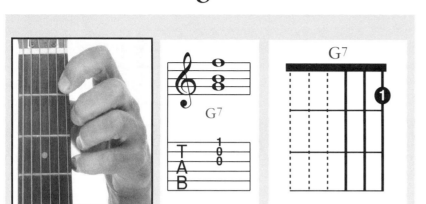 Track 22

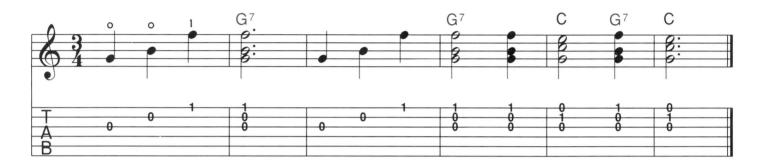

Down in the Valley Track 23

Down   in   the   val - ley,   val - ley   so

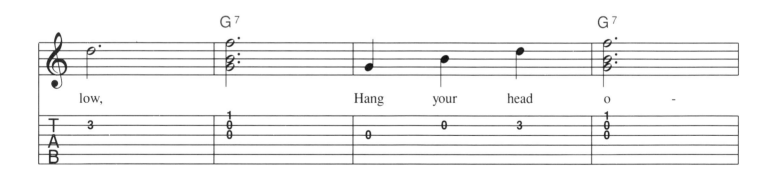

low,   Hang   your   head   o -

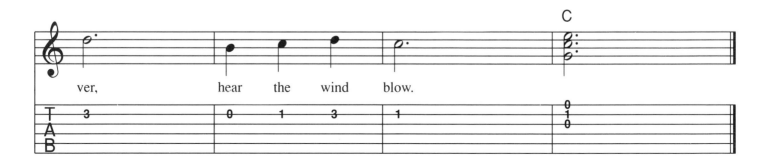

ver,   hear   the   wind   blow.

Mary Ann

 Track 24

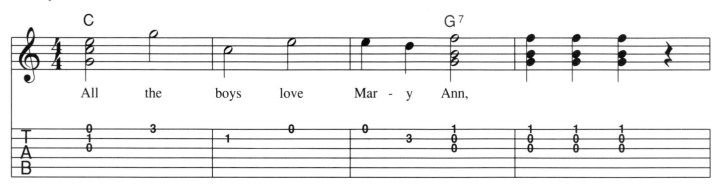

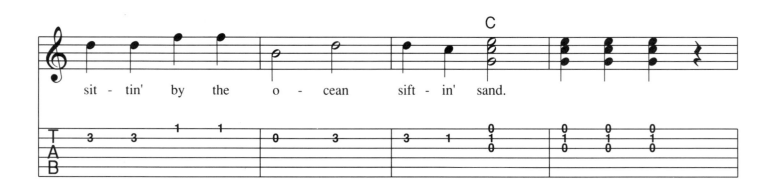

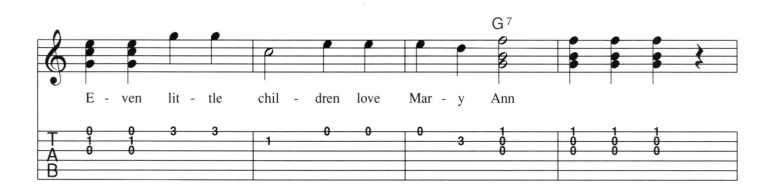

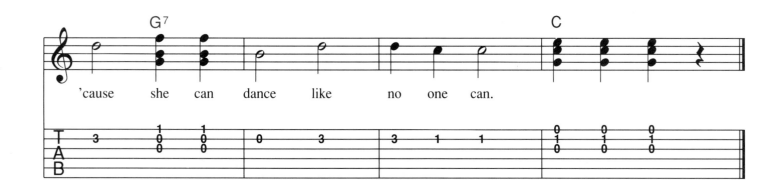

The Three-String G Chord Track 25

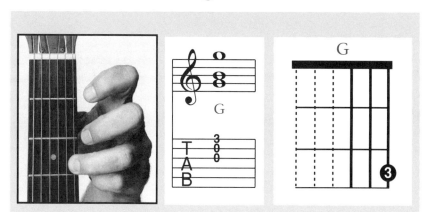

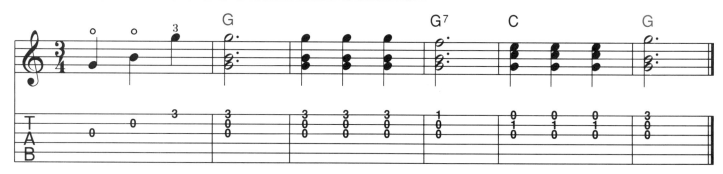

Rockin' with G and C Track 26

Fast Rock

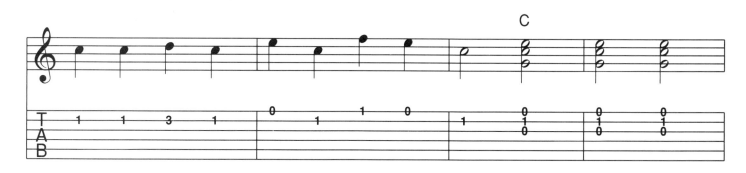

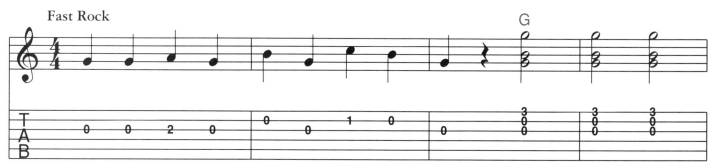

Notes on the Fourth String D   Track 27

OPEN STRING	2nd FRET	3rd FRET
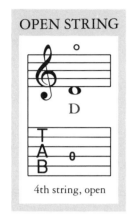	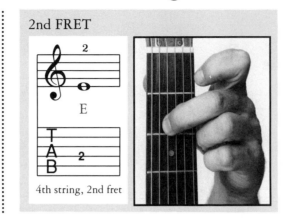	
4th string, open	4th string, 2nd fret	4th string, 3rd fret

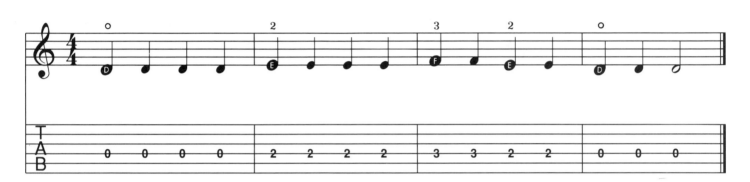

Reuben Reuben   Track 28

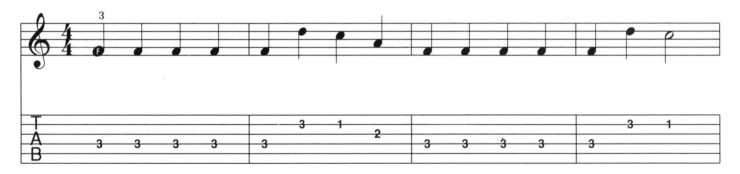

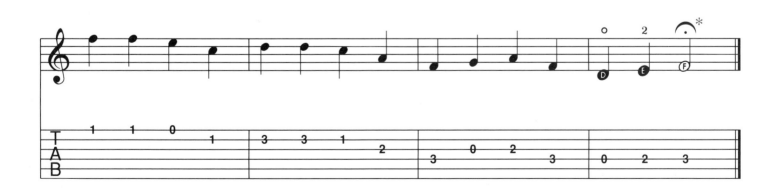

* HOLD SIGN (Fermata): This sign indicates that the time value of the note is lengthened at the discretion of the player (approximately 1 1/2 times).

Old MacDonald Had a Farm   Track 29

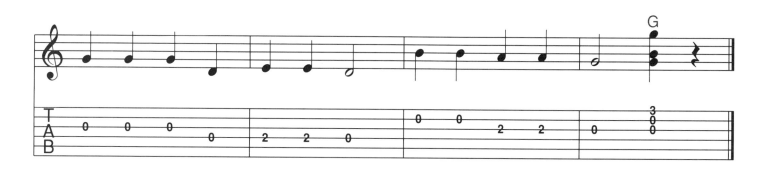

G Whiz   Track 30

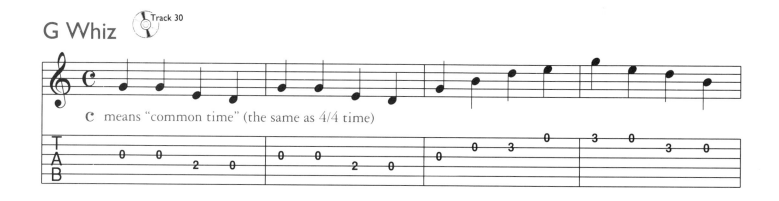

c means "common time" (the same as 4/4 time)

Goodnight Ladies Track 31

Not all guitar solos are played using only one form of the 3-note chords already learned. These songs use various combinations of 2- and 3-note chords.

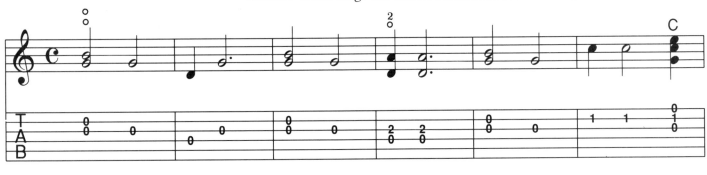

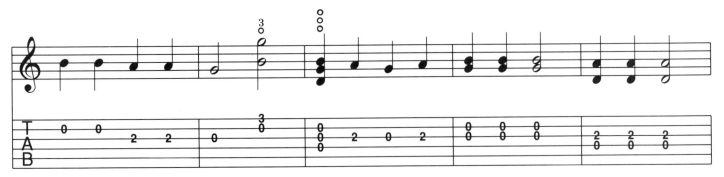

Daisy Bell  Track 32

(A Bicycle Built for Two)

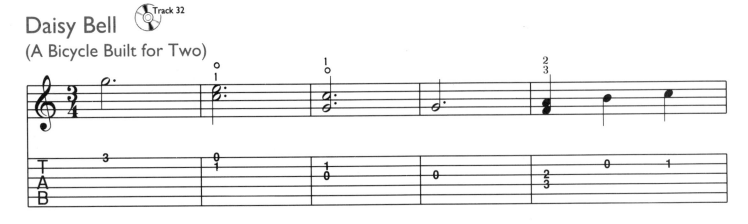

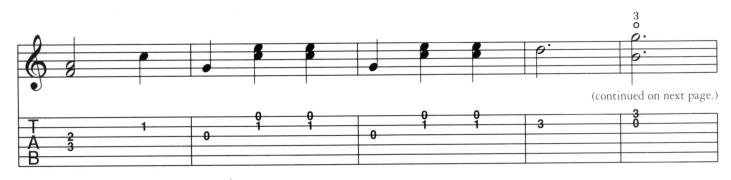

(continued on next page.)

Daisy Bell (cont'd.)

The Four-String G & G7 Chords

Track 33

The three-note G and G7 chords you have learned can be expanded to fuller and richer sounding four-note chords simply by adding the open 4th string.

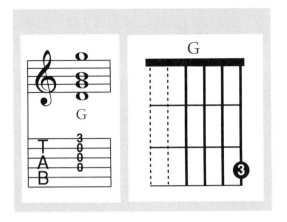

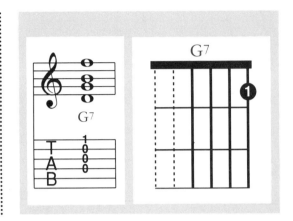

Rockin' the Chimes

The next song uses the four-note G and G7 chords. Sometimes the notes are played one at a time (called an arpeggio) instead of being played together (as a chord).

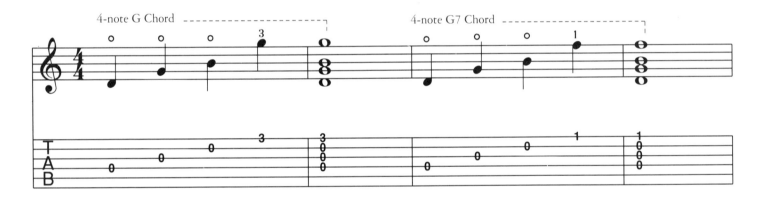

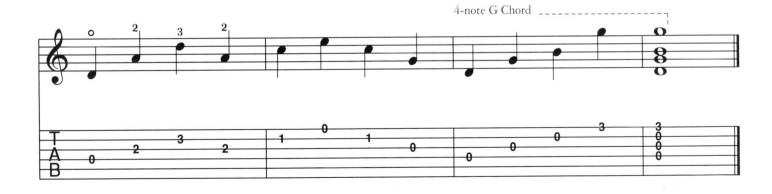

Laughing Troll

Track 34

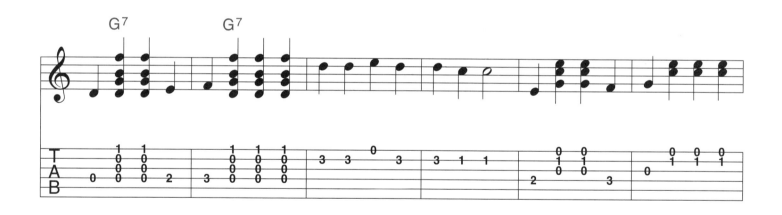

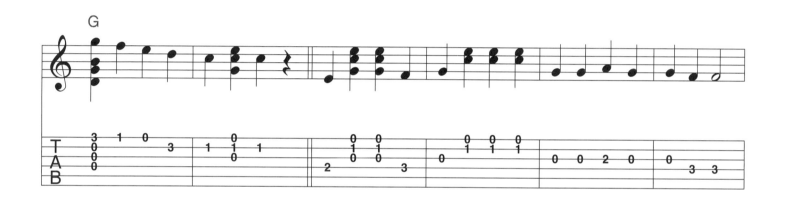

Notes on the Fifth String A 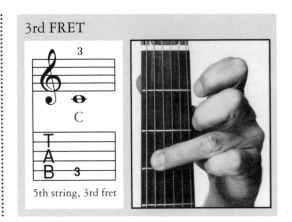 Track 35

OPEN STRING	2nd FRET	3rd FRET

A Leger Lines*	B	C
5th string, open	5th string, 2nd fret	5th string, 3rd fret

*The short line that extends the staff downwards is called a *leger* (pronounced ledger) line.

Peter Gray  Track 36

Boogie Style Track 37

Play this piece fast!

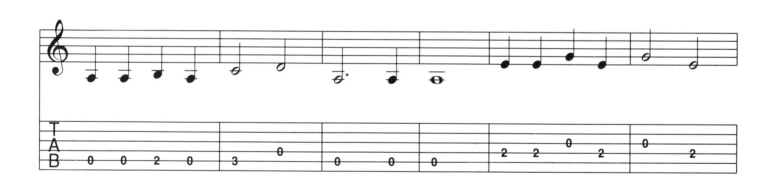

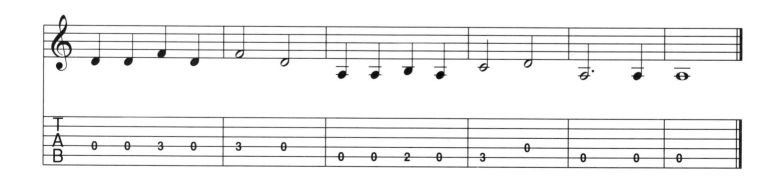

Introducing High A Track 38

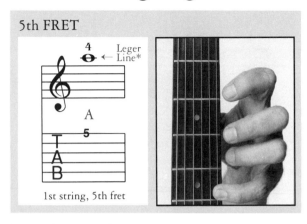

5th FRET

1st string, 5th fret

Notice that high A is played on the 5th fret, but the 4th finger is used. Slide your hand up the fret-board so the 4th finger can reach the 5th fret.

*Leger lines can also extend the staff upwards.

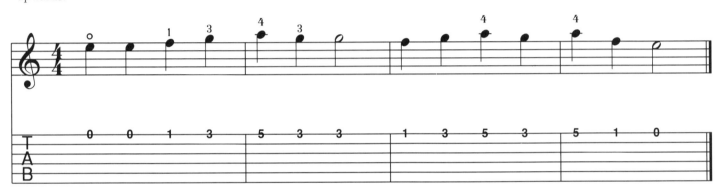

Rockin' in Dorian Mode Track 39

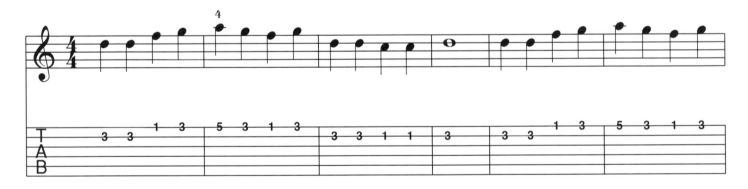

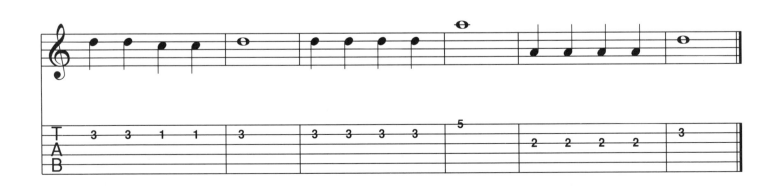

INCOMPLETE MEASURES

Not every piece of music begins on the first beat. Music sometimes begins with an incomplete measure, called the UPBEAT or PICKUP. If the upbeat is one beat, the last measure will sometimes have only three beats in 4/4, or two beats in 3/4 to make up for the extra beat at the beginning.

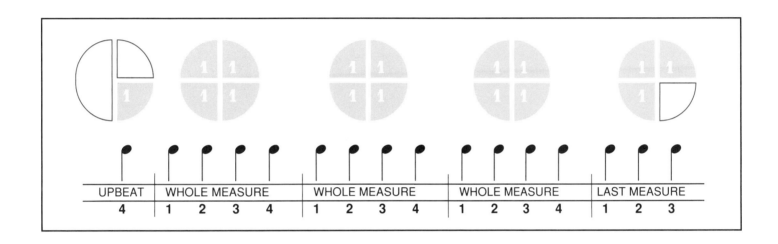

A-Tisket, A-Tasket   Track 40

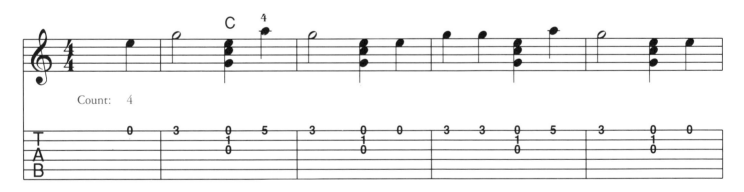

Count: 4

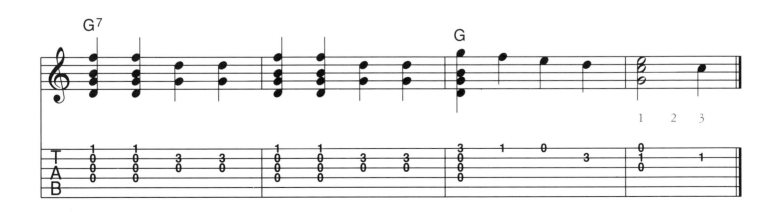

The Riddle Song

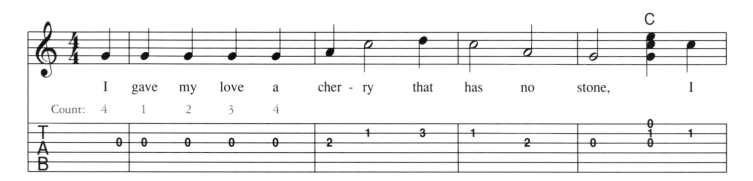

I gave my love a cher - ry that has no stone, I

Count: 4 1 2 3 4

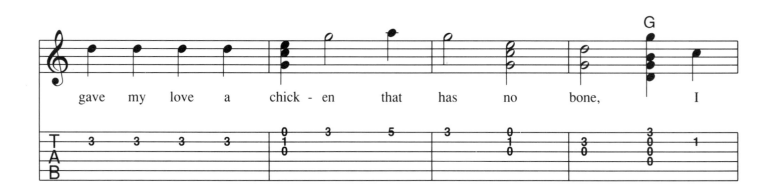

gave my love a chick - en that has no bone, I

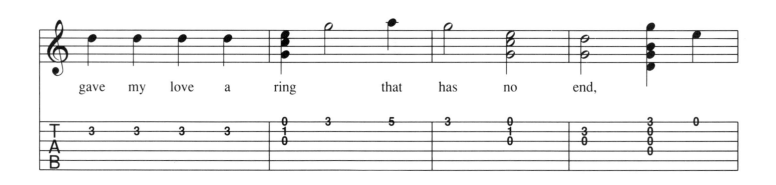

gave my love a ring that has no end,

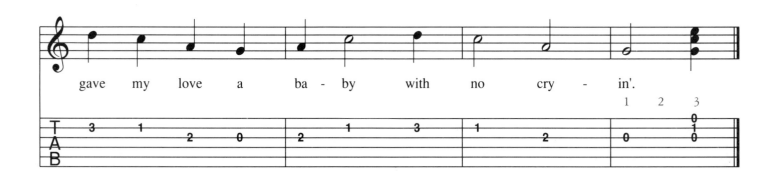

gave my love a ba - by with no cry - in'.

Notes on the Sixth String E

Track 42

OPEN STRING	1st FRET	3rd FRET

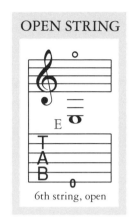

6th string, open

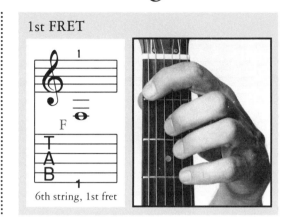

6th string, 1st fret

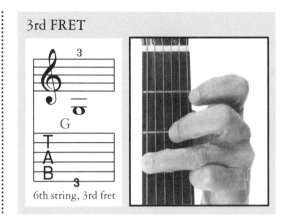

6th string, 3rd fret

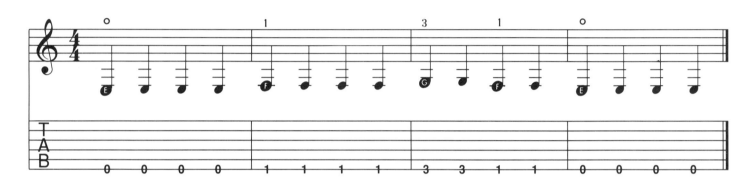

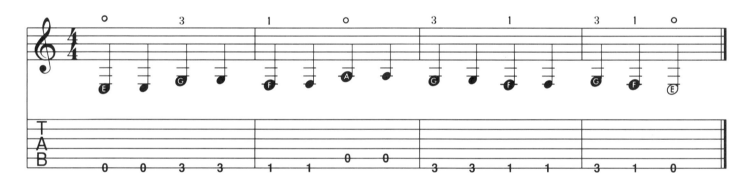

MINI MUSIC LESSON

THE NATURAL SCALE

Track 43

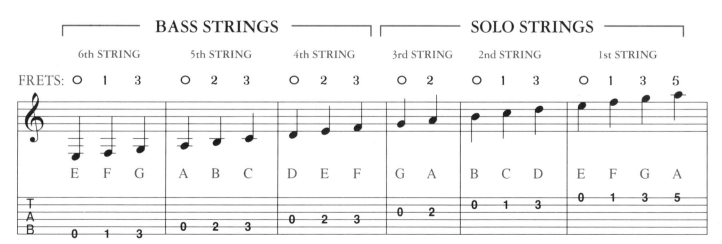

BASS STRINGS			SOLO STRINGS		
6th STRING	5th STRING	4th STRING	3rd STRING	2nd STRING	1st STRING

Silver Threads Among the Gold   Track 44

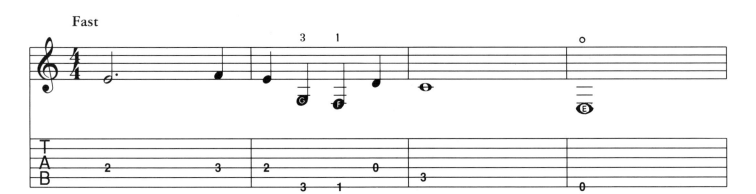

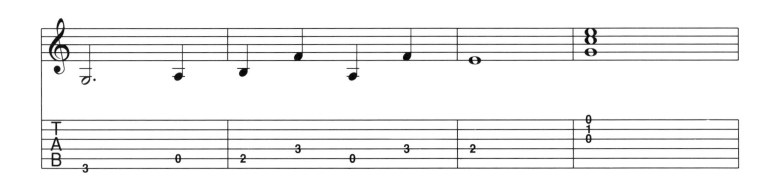

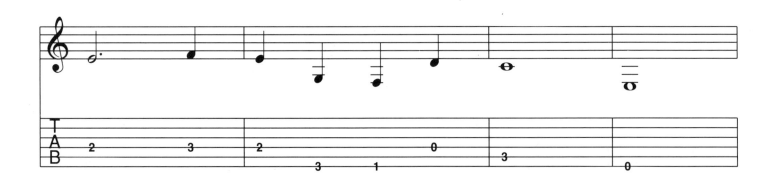

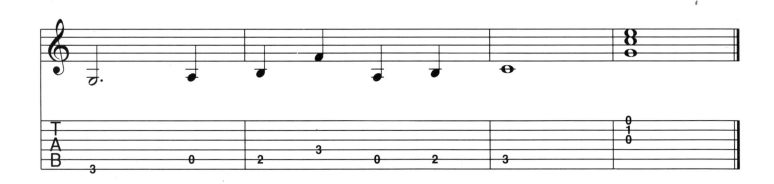

TEMPO SIGNS   Track 45

Tempo signs tell how fast or slow to play.

The three principal TEMPO SIGNS are: *Andante* (slow)   *Moderato* (moderately)   *Allegro* (fast)

say: on-*don*-tay   Mah-duh-*rah*-toe   Al-*lay*-grow

Three-Tempo Rock

Play three times: 1st time *Andante*, 2nd time *Moderato*, 3rd time *Allegro*.

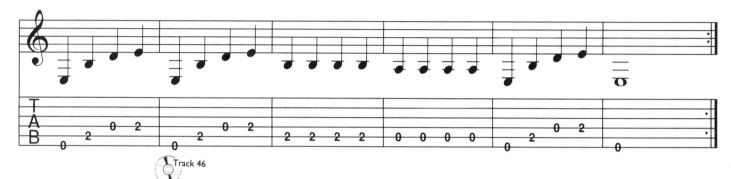

Plaisir d'amour
(The Joy of Love)

Track 46

You can do two things to get the most out of the next song arrangement. First, play accented notes (those marked with a >) a little louder than unmarked notes. Also, keep your finger(s) down where indicated. This will make your playing sound smoother and more professional.

Moderato

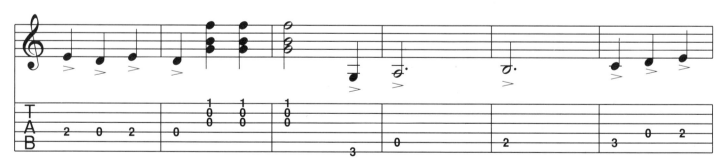

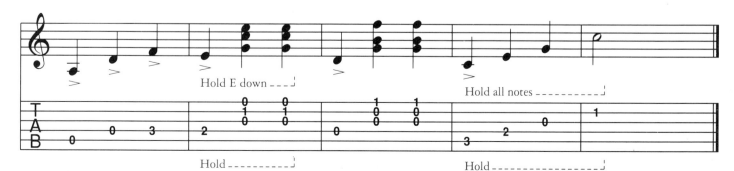

BASS-CHORD ACCOMPANIMENTS

 Track 47

A popular style of playing chord accompaniments in 4/4 time breaks the chord into two parts: a single bass note followed by a chord made up of the remaining notes. On the 1st beat play only the lowest note (called the bass note). Then play the rest of the chord (usually the three highest strings) on the 2nd, 3rd and 4th beats. The complete pattern is:

Bass note–chord–chord–chord.

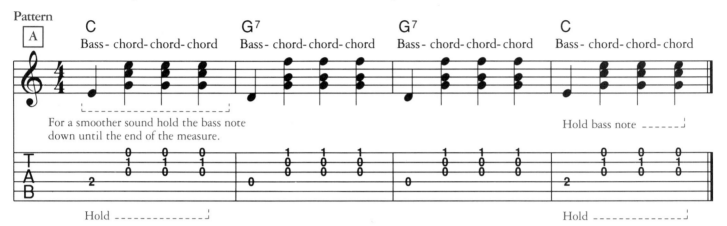

Another style of playing chord accompaniments in 4/4 time uses a bass note on the 1st and 3rd beats and three-string chords on the 2nd and 4th beats.

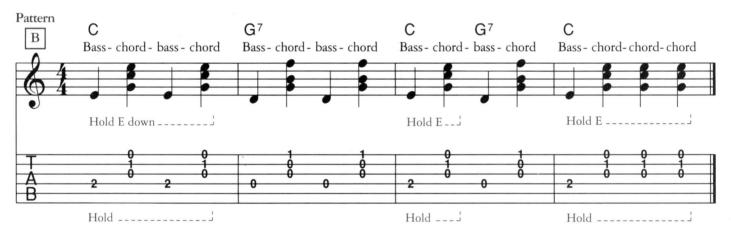

This style of playing chord accompaniments can be adapted to 3/4 time by playing a bass note on the 1st beat, and three-string chords on the 2nd and 3rd beats.

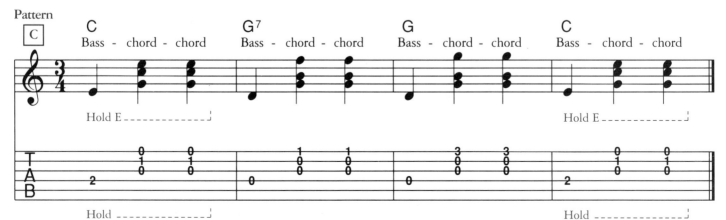

Can-Can
Duet

This famous melody from the opera *Orpheus in the Underworld* should be learned two different ways. First, play the solo part as written. Then find a friend to play the solo part or listen to it on your *Teach Yourself* recording while you play a chord accompaniment using either pattern A or B on page 42.

Allegro

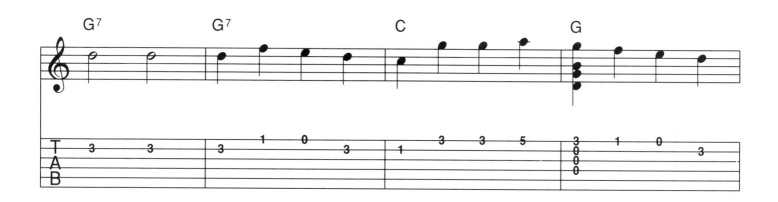

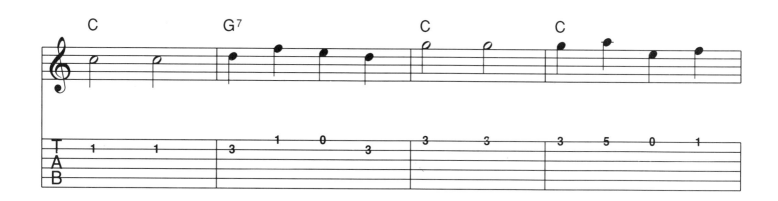

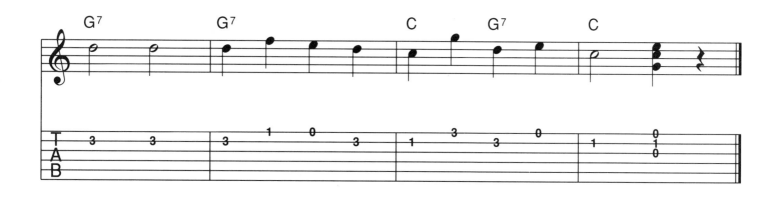

 DYNAMICS

Signs showing how SOFT or LOUD to play are called DYNAMICS. The principal dynamics are:

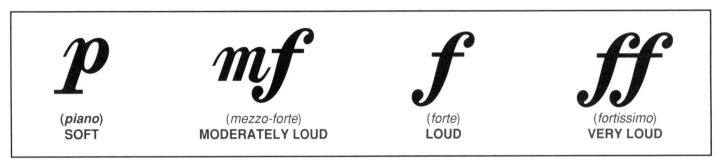

p	*mf*	*f*	*ff*
(*piano*) **SOFT**	(*mezzo-forte*) **MODERATELY LOUD**	(*forte*) **LOUD**	(*fortissimo*) **VERY LOUD**

Echo Song Track 49

Learn the solo part on the next song. If you wish to play it as a duet, use accompaniment pattern C described on page 42.

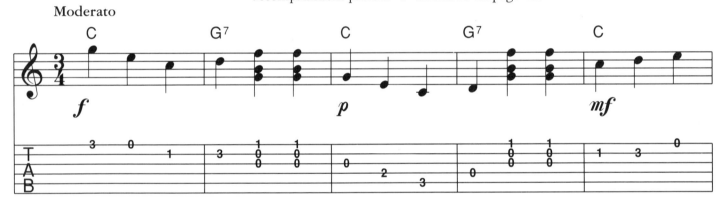

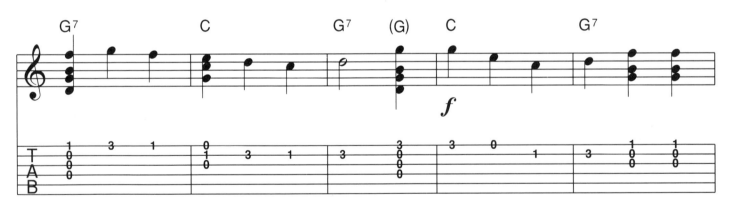

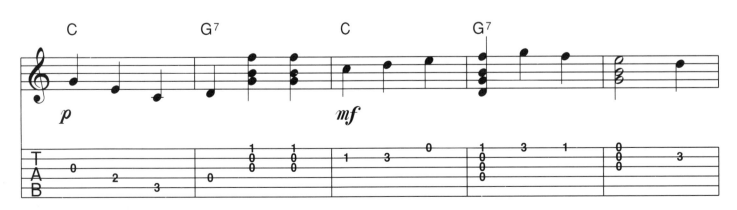

Echo Song (cont'd.)

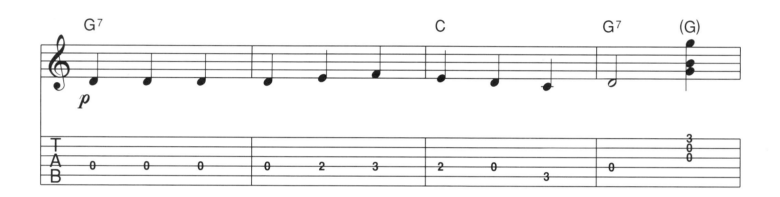

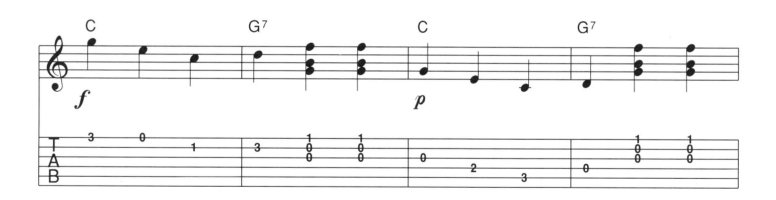

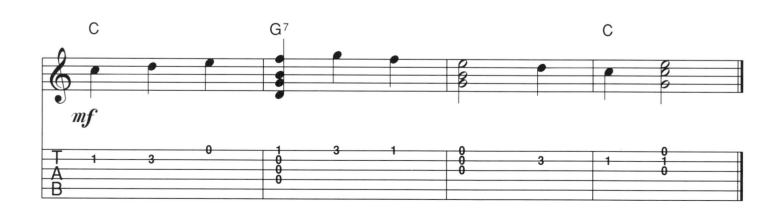

SIGNS OF SILENCE

QUARTER REST = 1 COUNT

HALF REST = 2 COUNTS

WHOLE REST = 4 COUNTS IN 4/4 TIME
3 COUNTS IN 3/4 TIME

An easy way to remember the difference between the half and whole rest is to think of the whole rest as being longer (or heavier) and so hangs below the line. The half rest is shorter (or lighter) and so sits on top of the line.

Give It A Rest Track 50

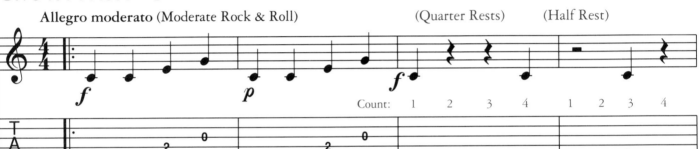

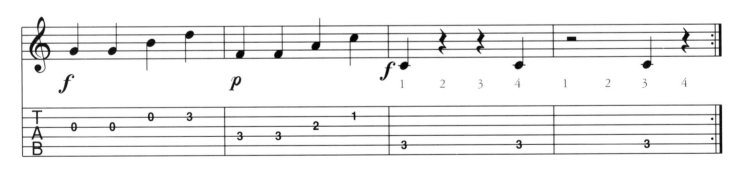

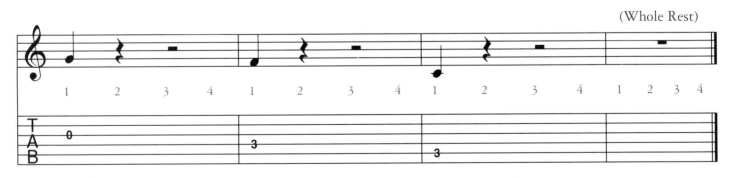

The Four-String C Chord

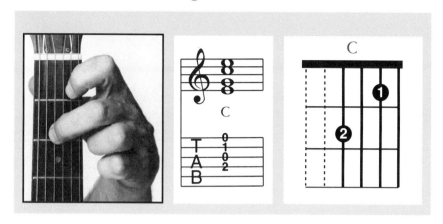

When the Saints Go Marching In

Track 51

Remember to play accented notes louder than unaccented ones.

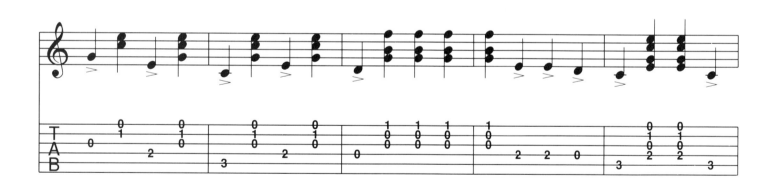

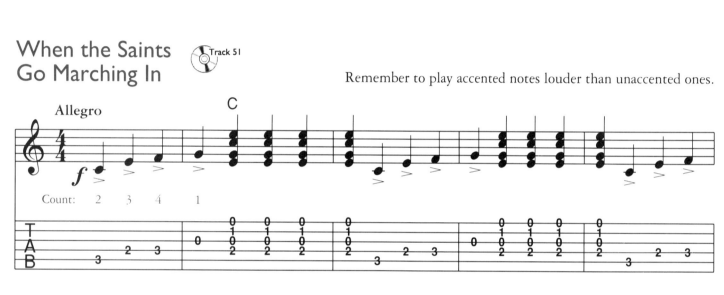

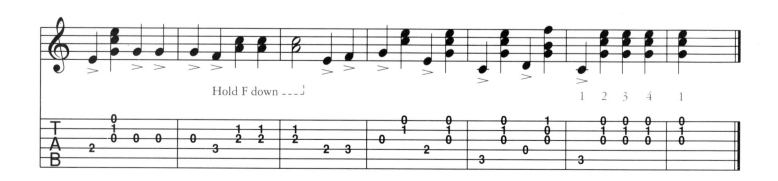

TIES Track 52

Ties are curved lines connecting two or more successive notes of the same pitch. When two notes are tied, the second one is not picked; its time value is added to the value of the first note. For example:

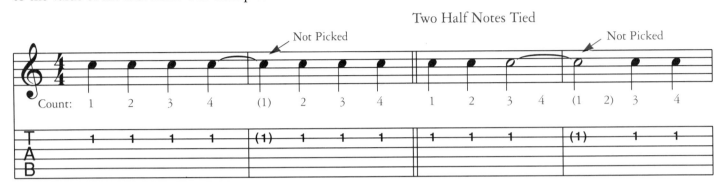

In tab notation, the tie is indicated by a parenthesis **(1)**—do not pick that note again.

The Sidewalks of New York Track 53
(East Side, West Side)

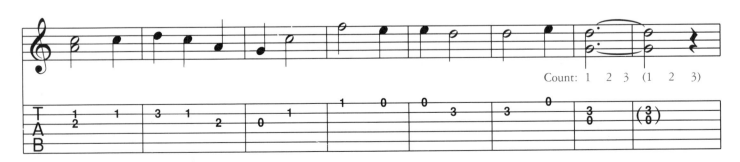

*Chords may also be tied.

The Sidewalks of New York (cont'd.)

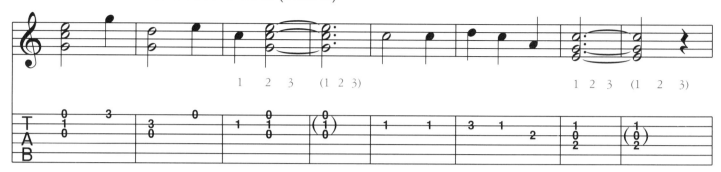

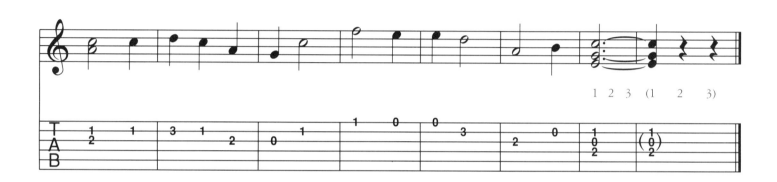

O Happy Day

Track 54

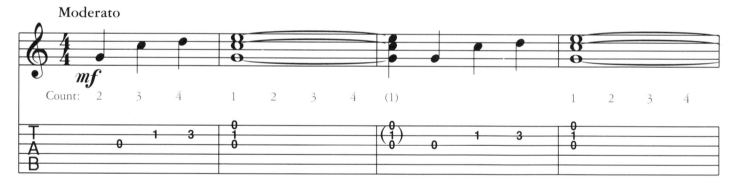

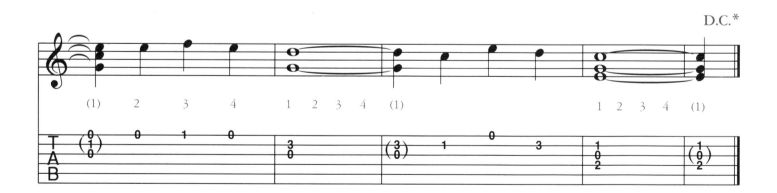

*D.C. = Da Capo [Dah *Cah*-po], an Italian expression meaning "From the beginning," which indicates that you should go back to the beginning and play through the piece a second time. Notice that the last measure contains only one beat. The 2nd, 3rd and 4th beats of this measure are made up at the beginning measure of the piece.

MORE BASS-CHORD ACCOMPANIMENTS (cont'd. from page 42)

When a piece is in 3/4 time, a popular style of chord accompaniment is found in the pattern: bass–chord–chord, chord–chord–chord. The bass note is the note that names the chord: C for the C chord, G for the G and G7 chords. Usually the bass note is also the lowest note in the chord. First play the bass note alone, then the rest of the chord on the 2nd and 3rd beats.

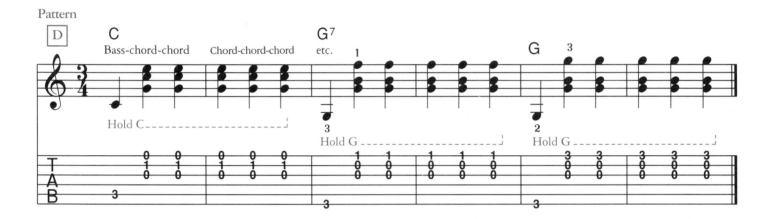

A variation on the above accompaniment uses a bass note on the 1st beat of each measure.

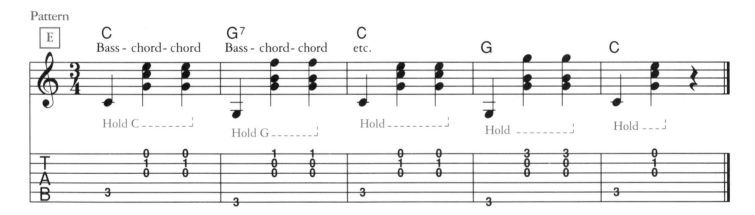

If a chord is repeated for two or more measures, alternate bass notes (any other note of the chord) can be used to get a greater variety of sound. In 4/4 time, you may use alternate bass notes every other measure or within measures.

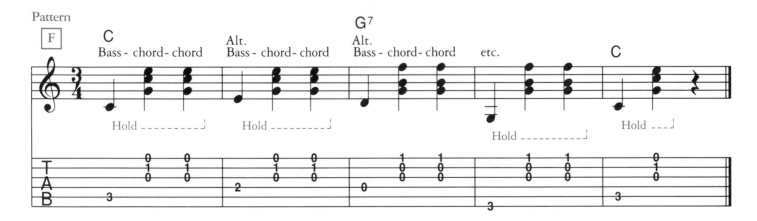

Cielito Lindo Track 56

Using the patterns you have just learned, play chord accompaniments (using bass and alternate bass notes) to this famous Mexican folk song. The melody is on your *Teach Yourself* recording. Then learn the melody as a guitar solo.

Allegro

Mexican Song

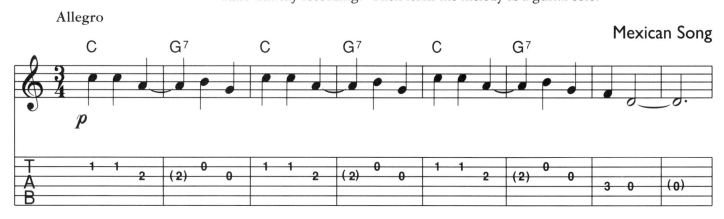

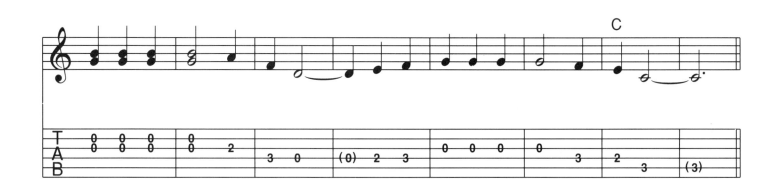

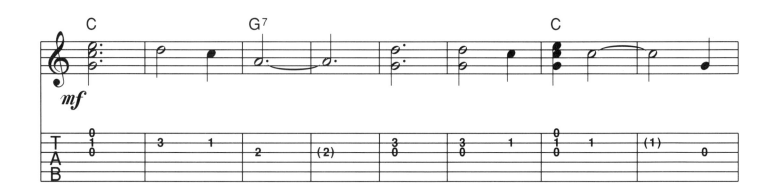

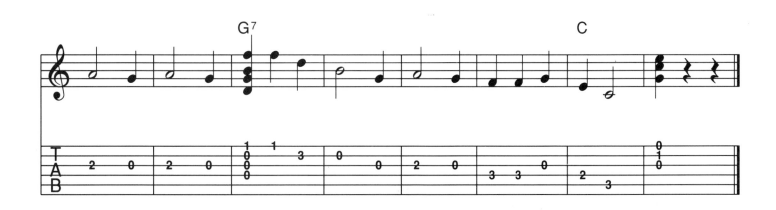

EIGHTH NOTES   Track 57

Eighth notes are black notes with a flag added to the stem ♪ or ♪ . Two or more eighth notes are written with connecting stems, ♫ or ♫ . The eighth rest ♪ .

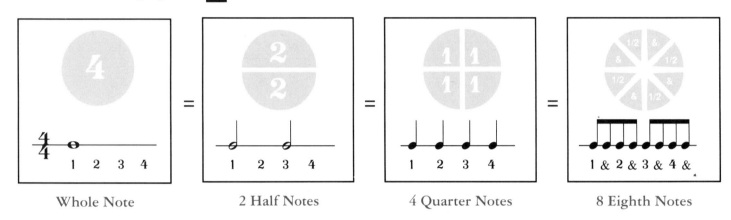

| Whole Note | 2 Half Notes | 4 Quarter Notes | 8 Eighth Notes |

Until now, you have been playing using downstrokes only. To be able to play more quickly, we will now use upstrokes.

Use alternating downstrokes ⊓
and upstrokes ∨ on eighth notes.

Count: 1 & 2 & 3 & 4 &   1 & 2 & 3 & 4 &

Eighth Note Rock   Track 58

Allegro moderato

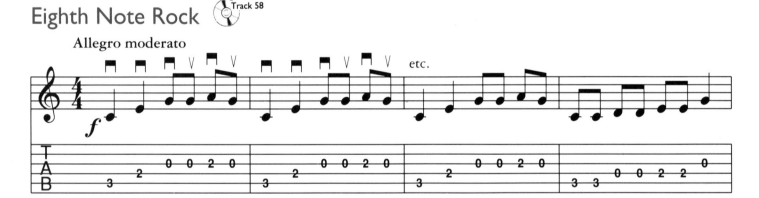

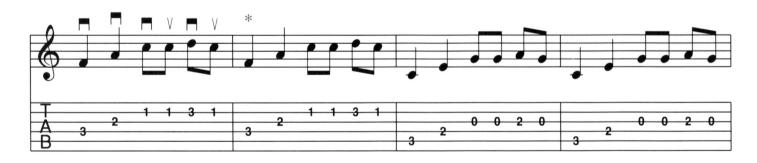

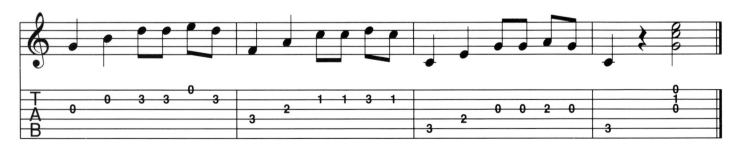

*Fill in the rest of the page with down and upstrokes.

Happy Birthday

Track 59

Mildred J. Hill & Patty S. Hill

Speed Drill

Track 60

Speed drills are for the development of technique and should be practiced daily. Start all speed drills slowly and be sure that each note is clear and distinct. On each repetition increase the tempo a little. We recommend you practice with a metronome to maintain an even tempo.

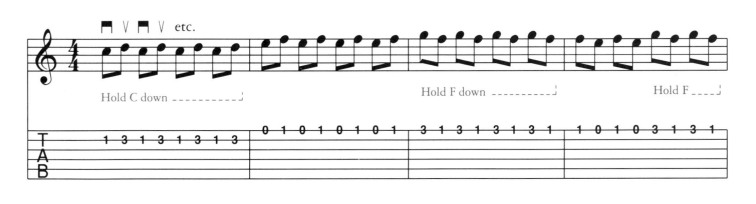

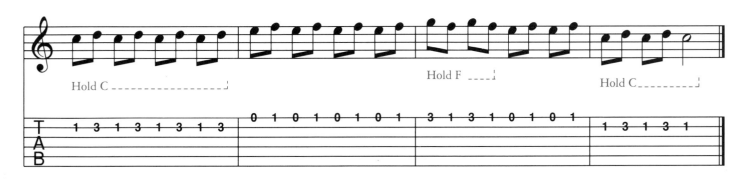

MINI MUSIC LESSON

SHARPS ♯, FLATS ♭ AND NATURALS ♮

The distance from one fret to the next fret, up or down is a HALF STEP.

TWO half steps make a WHOLE STEP.

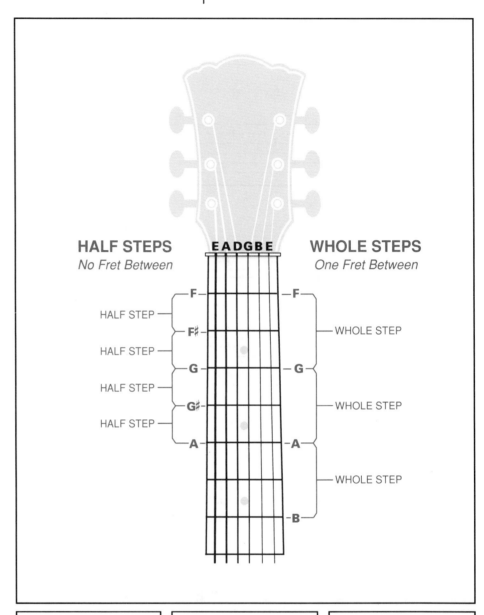

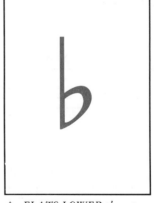

▲ SHARPS RAISE the note a half step. Play the next fret higher.

▲ FLATS LOWER the note a half step. If the note is fingered, play next fret lower. If the note is open, play the 4th fret of the next lower string except if that string is G (3rd string), then play the 3rd fret.

▲ NATURALS CANCEL a previous sharp or flat.

THE CHROMATIC SCALE   Track 61

The CHROMATIC SCALE is formed exclusively of HALF STEPS. Ascending, the CHROMATIC SCALE uses SHARPS (♯), but descending, uses FLATS (♭)

*When a sharped or flatted note appears more than once in the same measure, it is still played as a sharp or flat unless cancelled by a natural sign (♮).

The Four-String D7 Chord Track 63

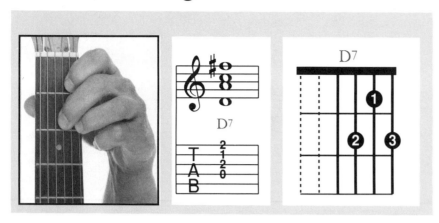

Hold fingers down.

*See footnote on page 55.

Four-Beat Blues Track 64

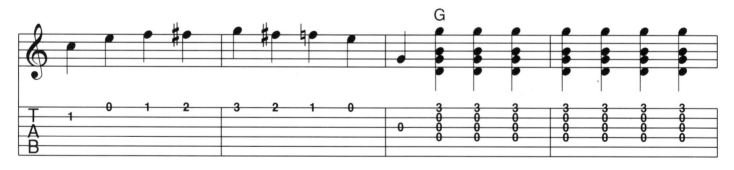

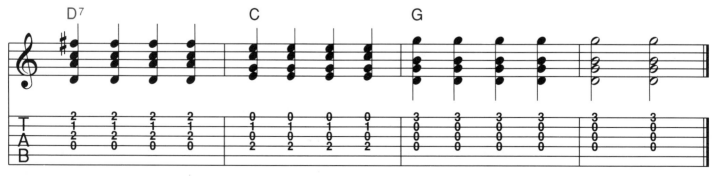

Rockin' the Bach Track 65

Adapted from a famous minuet by J.S. Bach

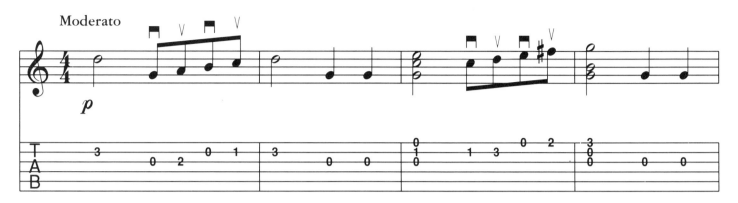

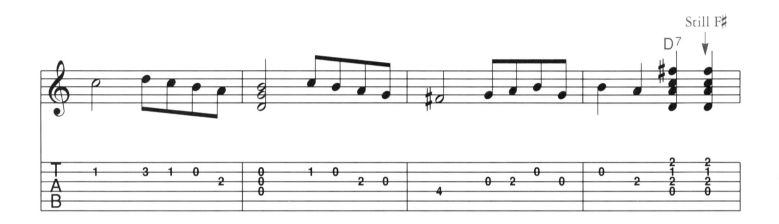

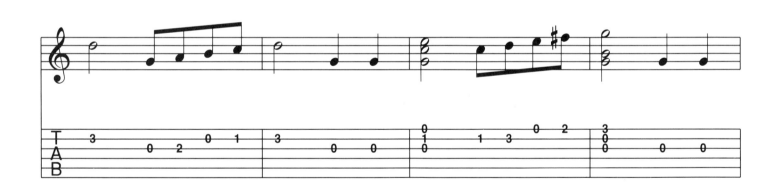

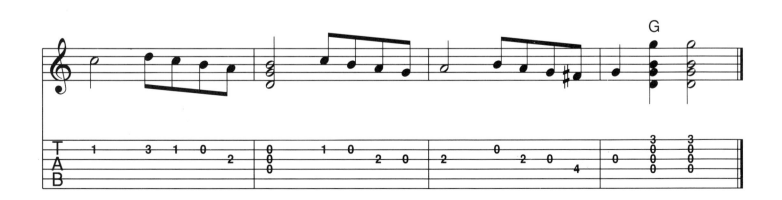

Amazing Grace Track 66

Learn the solo part and the accompaniment. Use pattern D, E or F on page 50.

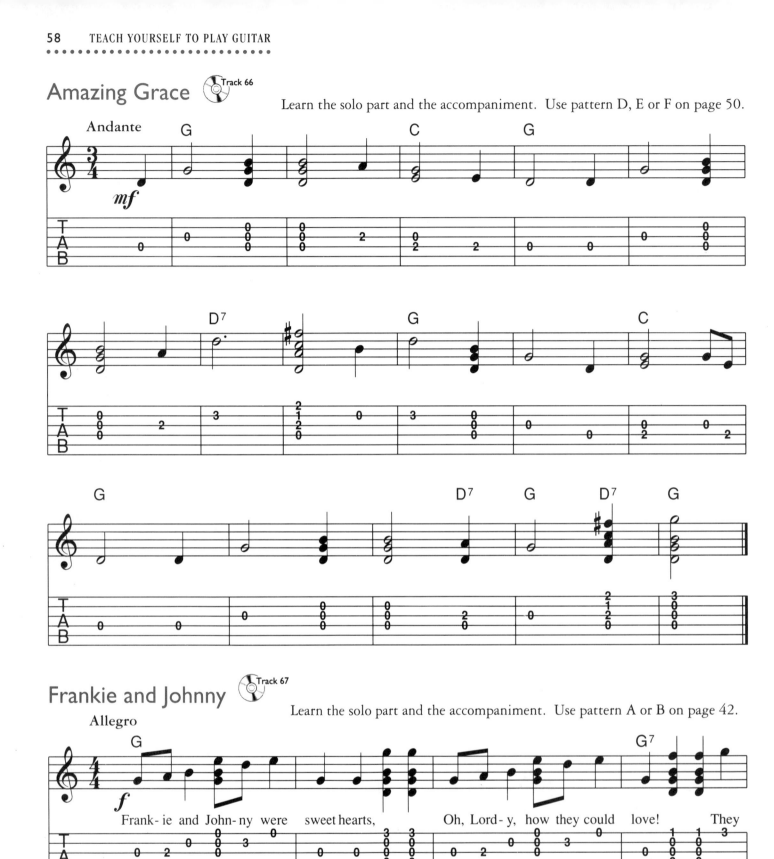

Frankie and Johnny Track 67

Learn the solo part and the accompaniment. Use pattern A or B on page 42.

Frank-ie and John-ny were   sweet hearts,   Oh, Lord-y, how they could   love!   They

swore   to   be   true   to each   oth - er   just   as   true   as   the   stars a - bove. He was   her

man, *f* but he done her wrong.

Pachelbel's Canon

Track 68

This 17th century piece has been used in many commercials and as the main theme in the movie *Ordinary People*.

Slow and stately

Hold E____ Hold C____ Hold__ Hold__ Hold__

*The sign ———————— or the word *crescendo* means gradually GROW LOUDER

The sign ———————— or the word *diminuendo* means gradually GROW SOFTER

THE MAJOR SCALE

A scale is a series or succession of tones. All major scales are made of eight tones, which ascend in alphabetical order. The major scale always follows this pattern of alternating whole and half steps:

C Major Scale

The Octave Note

This scale has eight notes. The highest note, having the same letter-name as the first note is called the *octave* note.

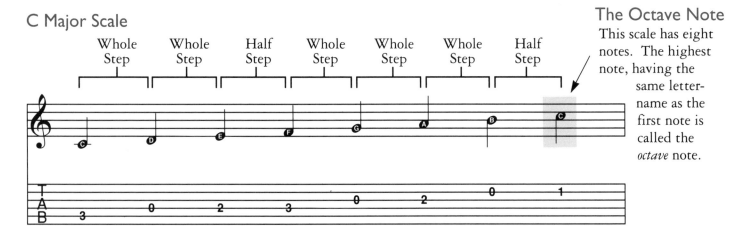

It is easier to visualize whole steps and half steps on a piano keyboard. Notice that there are whole steps between every white key except E–F and B–C.

Whole Steps—One Key Between
Half Steps–No Key Between

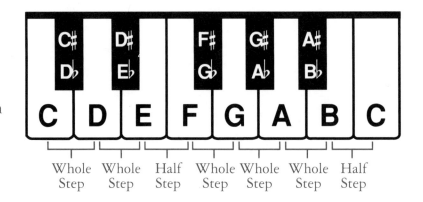

The MAJOR SCALE may be built starting on ANY NOTE—natural, sharp or flat. Using this pattern, write a MAJOR SCALE, starting on G:

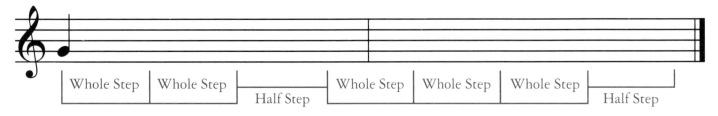

CHECK: Are the notes in alphabetical order? Did you give the 7th note a sharp?

Write a MAJOR SCALE, starting on F:

CHECK: Are the notes in alphabetical order? Did you give the 4th note a flat?

KEY SIGNATURES

The Key of C Major:

A piece based on the C MAJOR SCALE is in the KEY OF C MAJOR. Since there are no sharps or flats in the C scale, any sharps or flats occurring in a piece in the key of C major are called *accidentals*.

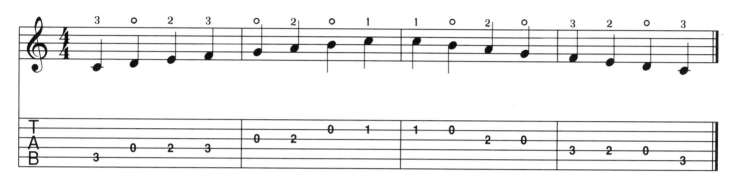

The Key of G Major:

A piece based on the G major scale is in the key of G major. Since F is sharp in the G scale, every F will be sharp in the key of G major. Instead of adding a sharp every time an F appears in a piece, the sharp is indicated at the beginning, in the key signature. Sharps or flats shown in the key signature remain effective throughout the piece.

Key Signature
One Sharp (F♯)

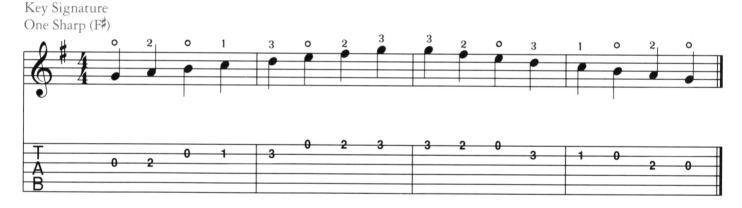

The Key of F Major:

A piece based on the F major scale is in the key of F major.

Key Signature
One Flat (B♭)

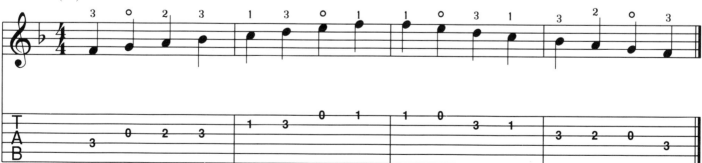

If sharps, flats or naturals not shown in the key signature occur in the piece, they are called *accidentals*. Accidentals are effective only for the measures in which they appear. The three scales shown above should be practiced every day. Students who do this should have little difficulty playing selections written in C major, G major and F major.

This Land Is Your Land Track 69

Woody Guthrie

First learn the solo part, then the accompaniment using pattern B on page 42. Keep in mind that this arrangement is in the key of G; all the F's are played as F♯ except when preceded by a natural (♮). This song has become popular all over the world. The lyrics are changed to fit each country.

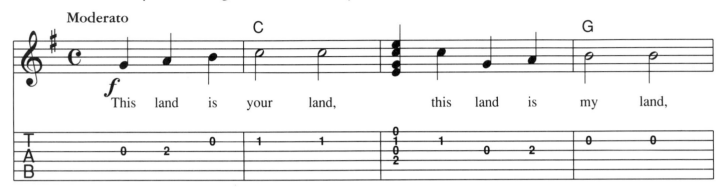

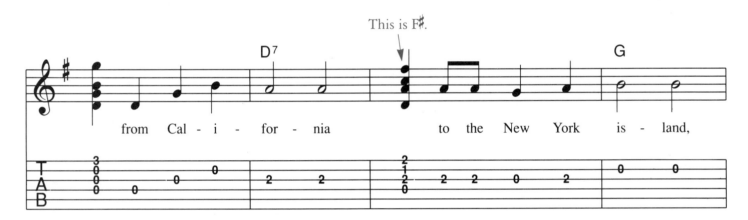

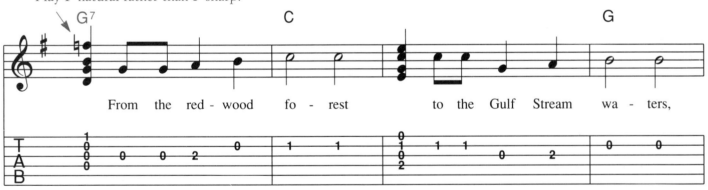

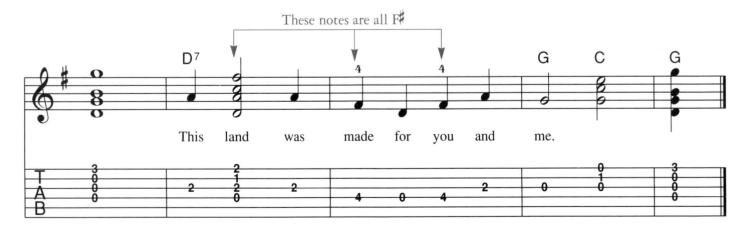

© Copyright 1956 (renewed), 1958 (renewed) and 1970 Ludlow Music, Inc., New York, NY. Used by Permission.

La Bamba

 Track 70

Allegro

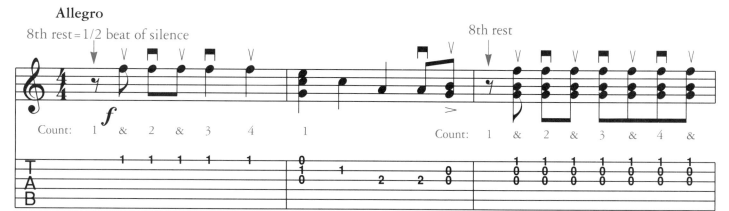

Repeat and fade

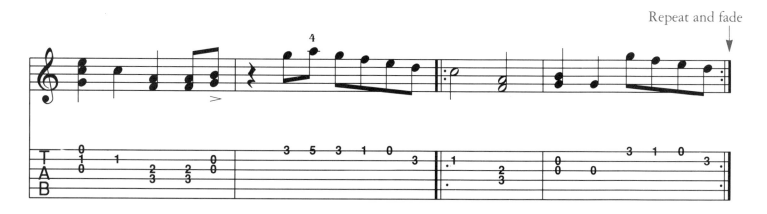

*See footnote on page 20 concerning repeat signs.

 INTRODUCING DOTTED QUARTER NOTES

A dot increases the length of a note by one-half.

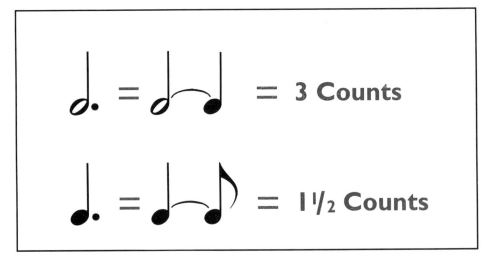

Preparatory Drill

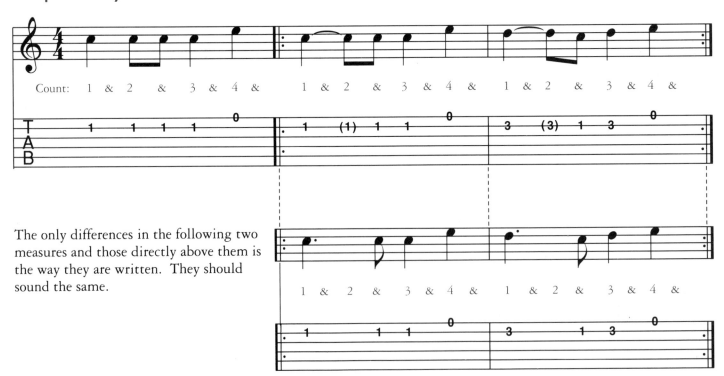

The only differences in the following two measures and those directly above them is the way they are written. They should sound the same.

Auld Lang Syne    Track 71

Rockabilly Bass Line  Track 72

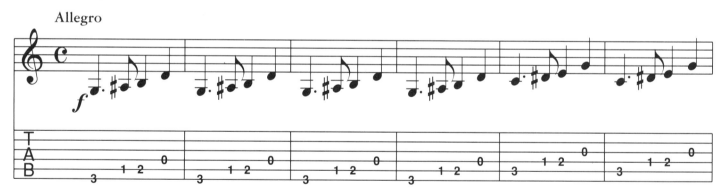

Hava Nagila  Track 73

Israeli Folk Song

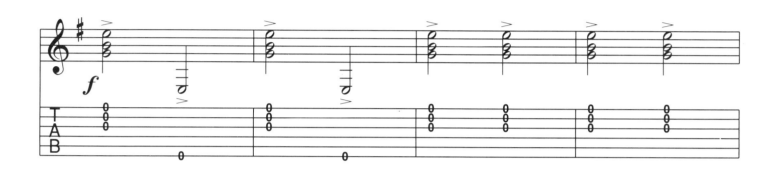

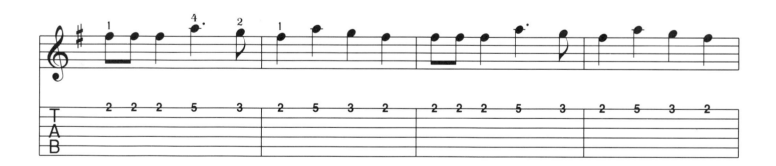

*High B; 1st string, 7th fret.

ADVANCED TABLATURE TECHNIQUES Track 74
Used in Rock, Heavy Metal, Blues, Country and Jazz

One of the problems with traditional music notation in relation to the guitar is that it doesn't show how the music is to be played or where on the neck the note should be fingered. Tablature enables the guitarist to play more precisely by the use of special symbols that we will introduce to you now. Through these symbols you will be able to see when a note should be "bent" up, when to "slide" from one note to another, when to "hammer-on" or "pull-off" and much more. Tablature enables the guitarist to see a graphic representation of the exact technique that the music requires.

Bends

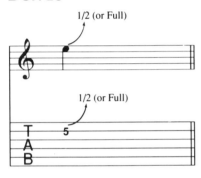

When you see this symbol, pick the note shown and then bend the string, by pushing it up until the desired pitch is reached. We will start with a 1/2 bend. This means you bend the note up one half step —the equivalent in tone to one fret up. At first it may be somewhat difficult to bend the string but the more you practice it the stronger your fingers will become. The farther up the neck you play bends, the easier it is to bend the string.

Bend Exercise #1

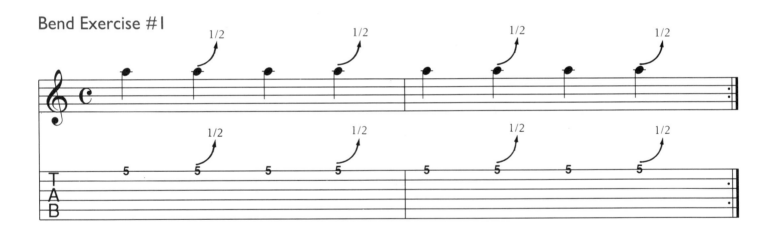

Bend Exercise #2

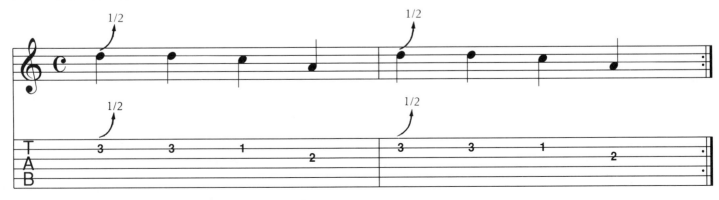

Pick Bend & Release

Track 75

Pick the first (lower) note, bend the string up one half step to sound the second (higher) note, then straighten the string to sound the original (lower) note again. Pick only the first note.

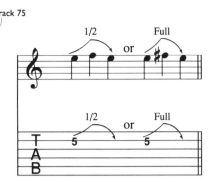

Pick Bend & Release Exercise #1

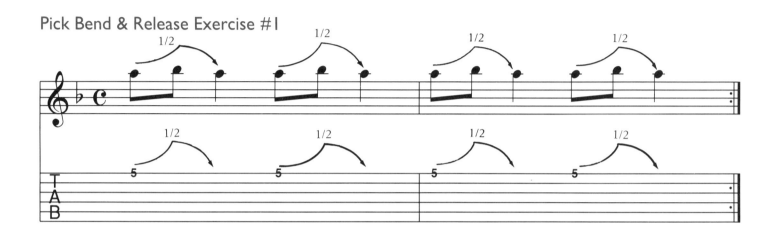

Pick Bend & Release Exercise #2

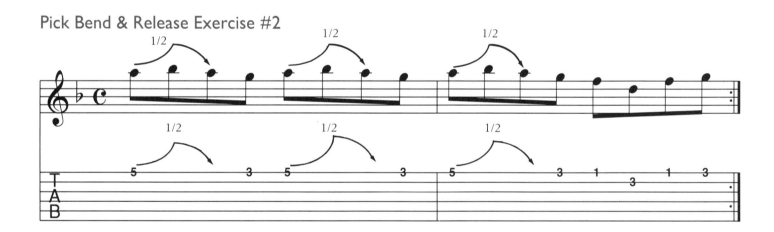

Bend and Pick Bend & Release Exercise #3

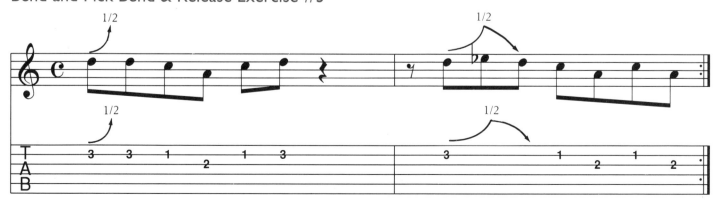

Hammer-On   Track 76

Pick the first (lower) note, then hammer-on (tap down firmly on the fret board) the second (higher) note with another finger from the left hand. Pick only the first note. The sound of the second note is made by the hammer-on. These notes are always played on the same string.

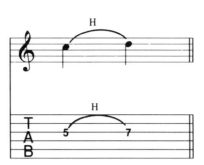

Hammer-on Exercise #1

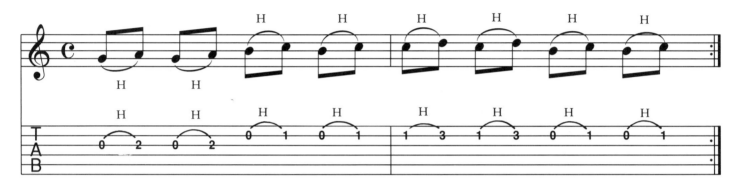

Hammer-on Exercise #2

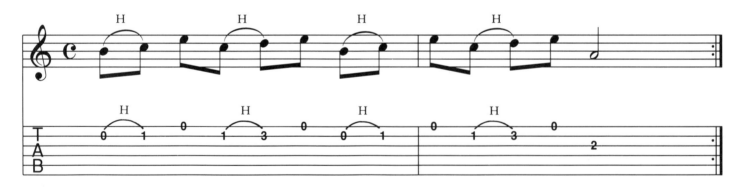

Hammer-on Exercise #3

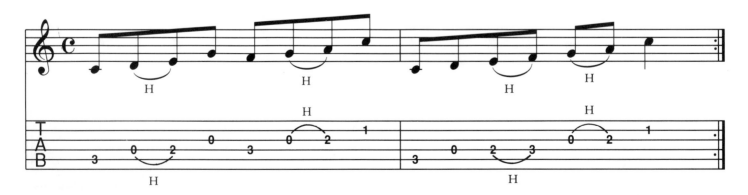

Pull-Off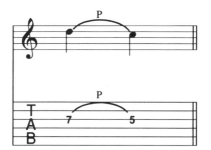

When pulling-off to an open string note, pick only the first (higher) note, then pull-off (raise-up) the first finger of the higher note. The sound of the open string is made by the pull-off from the first note.

Pull-off Exercise #1

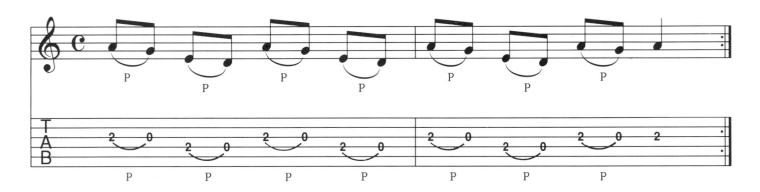

Place both fret fingers on the two notes to be played. Pick the first (higher) note, then pull-off (raise-up) the fret finger of the higher note while keeping the lower note fretted. Pick only the first note. The sound of the second note is made by the pull-off from the first note.

Pull-off Exercise #2

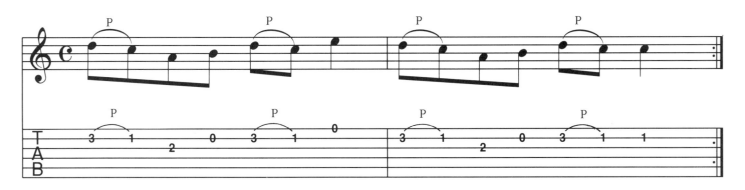

Hammer-on and Pull-off Exercise #3

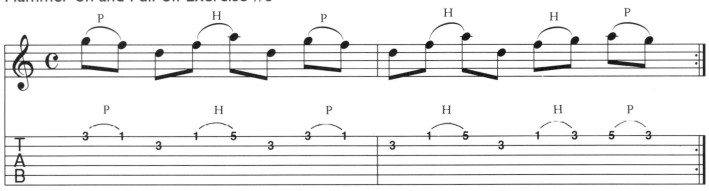

Slides 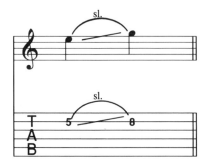 Track 78

Pick the first (lower) note, then slide the fret finger up to sound the second (higher) note. The second (higher) note is not picked.

Slide Exercise #1

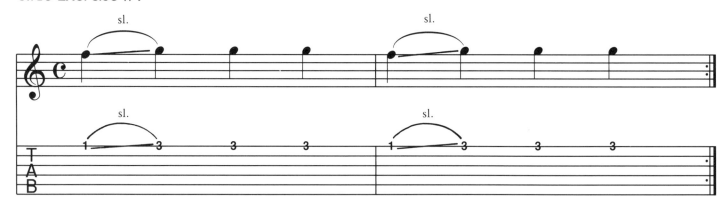

Slide Exercise #2

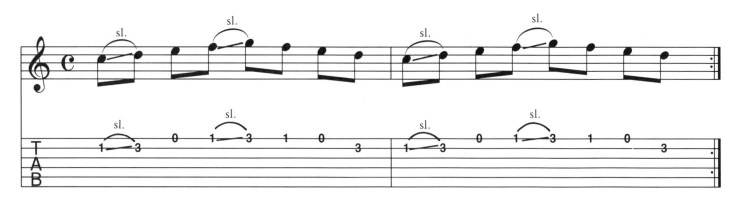

Hammer-on, Pull-off & Slide

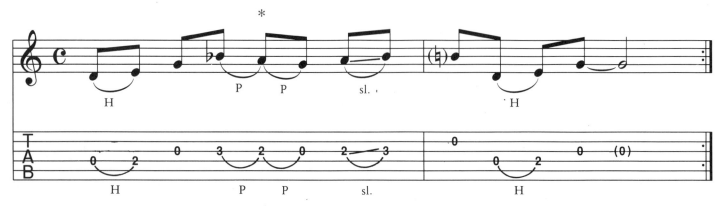

*When playing two consecutive pull-offs, pick the first note, then pull-off to sound the second note—then pull-off to sound the third note. Pick the string only once.

Palm Mute Track 79

The note is partially muted by the right (pick) hand lightly touching the string or strings just before the bridge with the "heel" of the hand. The note is then picked, giving it a muffled sound. The key is not to press too hard with the right hand as this will overly silence the note.

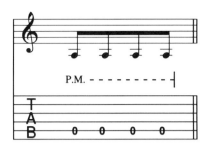

Palm Mute Exercise #1

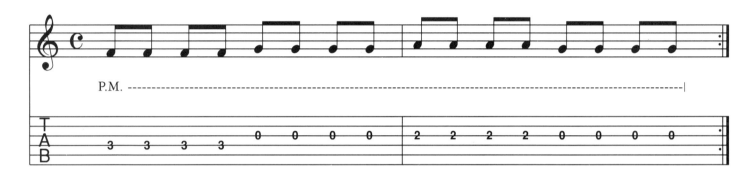

Palm Mute Exercise #2

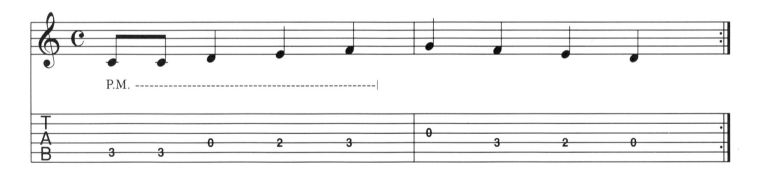

Hammer-on, Pull-off, Slide and Palm Mute

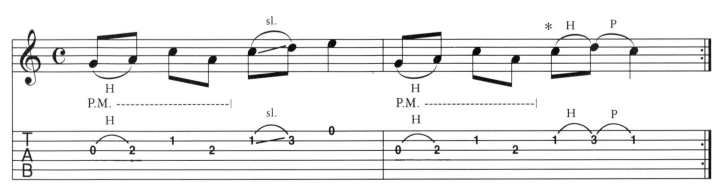

*Pick only the first note.

TABLATURE LICKS

A lick is a pattern or series of notes which is commonly used as a basis for soloing. On the next few pages we are going to introduce you to different styles of music through the use of licks. These licks should help you understand how tablature and these new techniques can affect your playing and the sounds you can get out of your guitar.

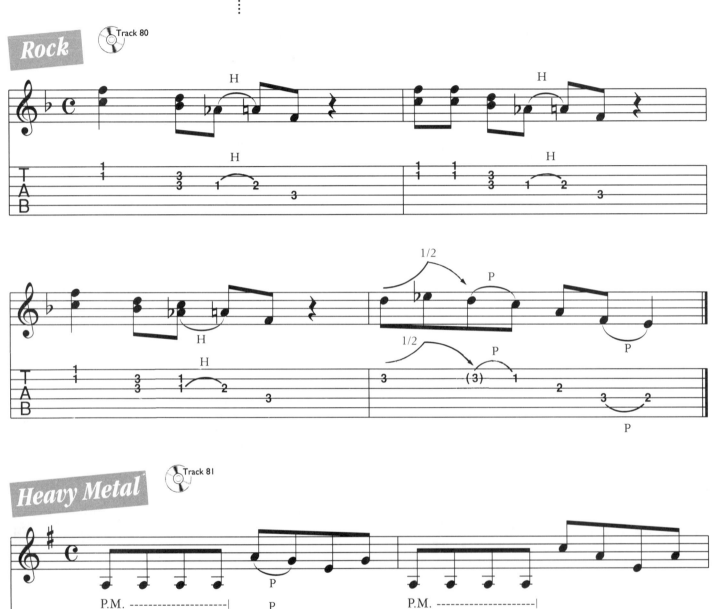

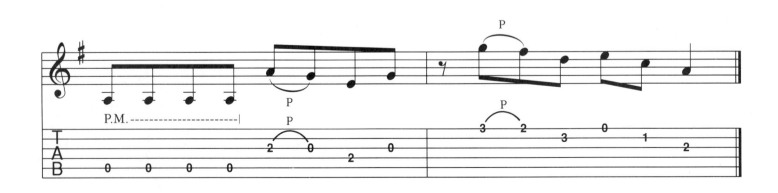

Blues

Track 82

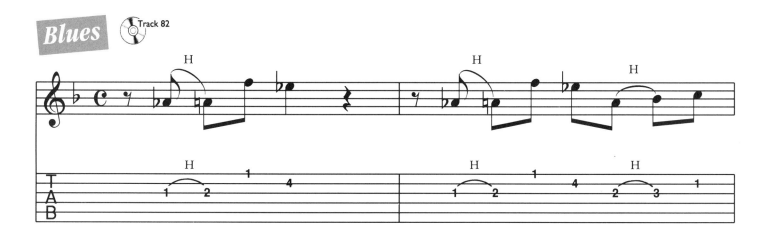

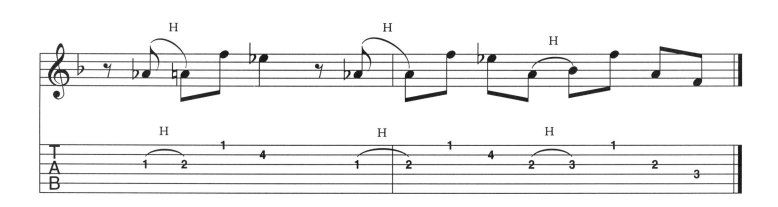

Country

Track 83

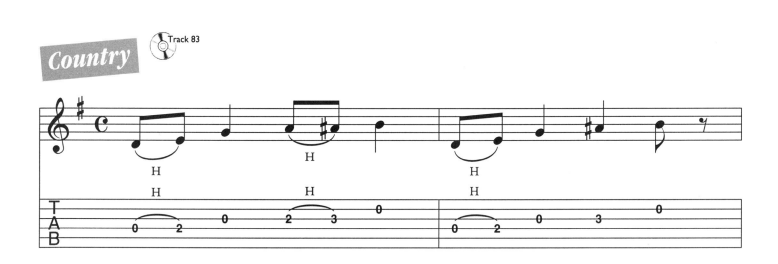

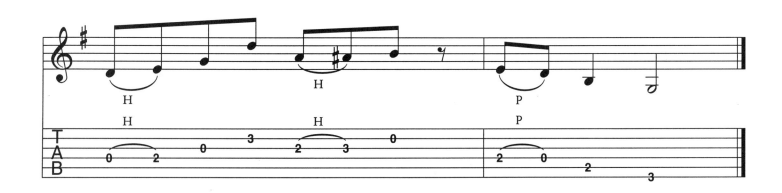

Jazz

Track 84

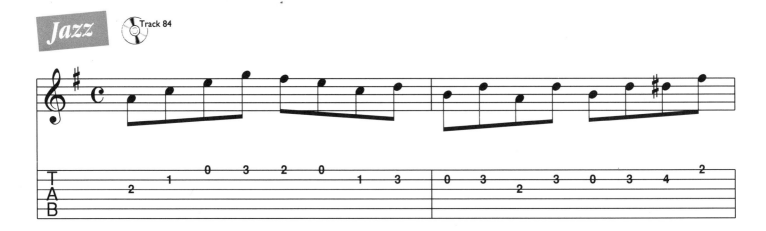

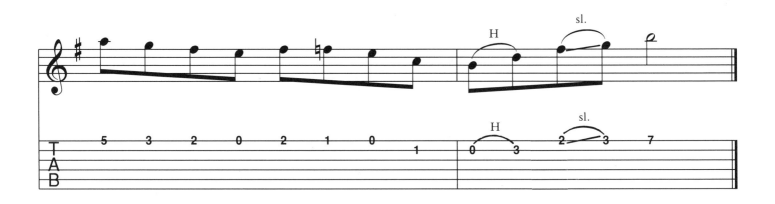

Jazz-Rock

Track 85

DICTIONARY OF TABLATURE TECHNIQUES

Bends

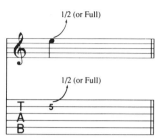

One- or Two-Note Up Bend: Pick the first note, then bend the string to sound up either one or two half steps.

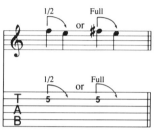

One- or Two-Note Down Bend: Pick the first (bent) note, then straighten the string to sound the lower (second) note.

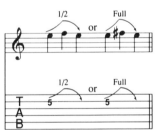

Pick Bend and Release: Pick the first note, bend the string up one or two half steps to sound the higher (second) note, then straighten the string to sound the original (first) note again. Pick only the first note.

Bend and then Pick: Bend the first note up one or two half steps before picking it. This is usually followed by a down bend.

Mute

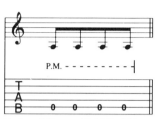

Palm Mute (P.M.): The note is partially muted by the pick hand by lightly touching the string or strings just before the bridge.

Slides

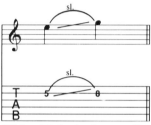

Slide: Pick the lower (first) note, then slide the fret finger up to sound the higher (second) note. The higher note is not picked again.

Slide and Pick: Same as the slide except the higher note is also picked.

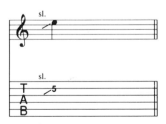

Long Slide: Strike the note during the slide up to the desired note.

Tapping

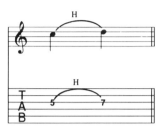

Hammer-on: Pick the lower (first) note, then hammer-on (tap down on the fret board) the higher (second) note with another finger. Pick only the first note. These notes are always played on the same string.

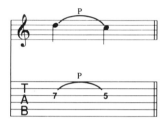

Pull-off: Place both fret fingers on the two notes to be played. Pick the higher (first) note, then pull-off (raise up) the fret finger of the higher note while keeping the lower note fretted. Pick only the first note.

Vibrato

Vibrato: Pick the string as the fret finger or a tremolo bar rapidly rolls back and forth or bends up and down, making the note sound slightly higher and lower. An exaggerated vibrato can be achieved by rolling the fret finger a greater distance.

GUITAR NOTE CHART
The number in the black circle on the fingerboard indicates the correct fingering.

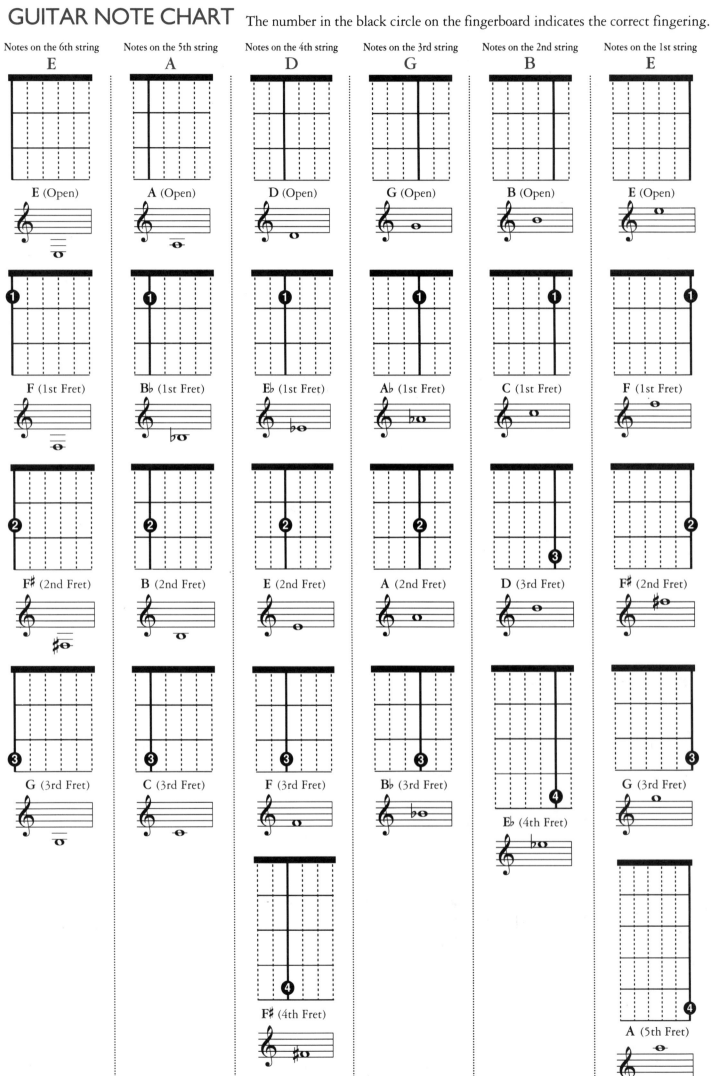

Magic Chord Accompaniment Guide

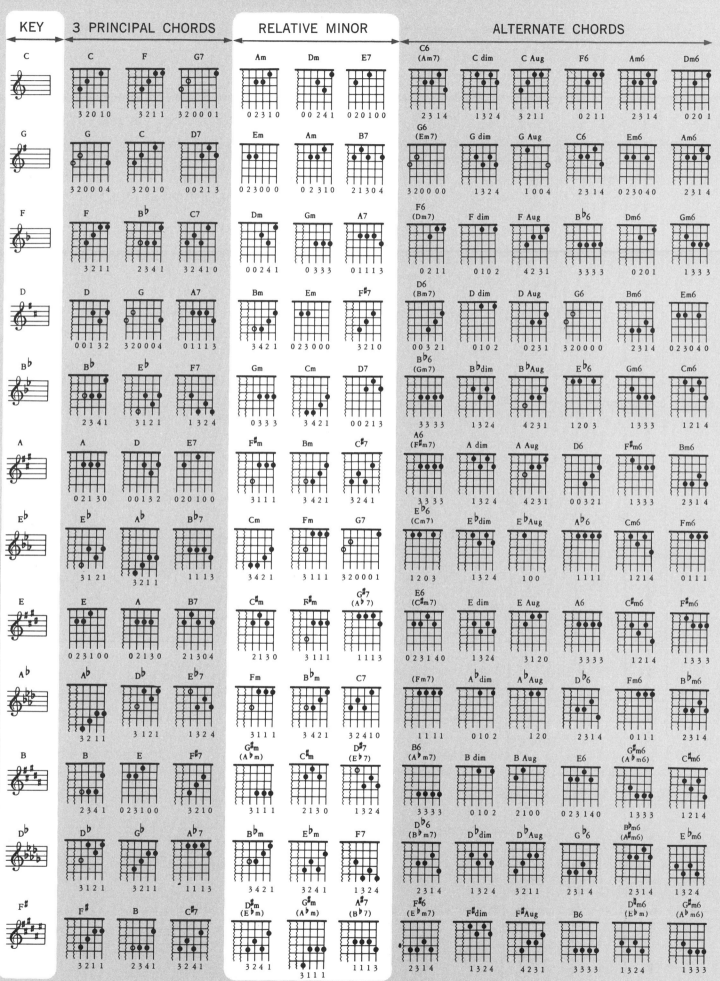

o = in chord diagram indicates optional fingering.

} = string not to be played.

Numbers under diagram indicate fingering:

O = Open
1 = Index finger   3 = Ring finger
2 = Middle finger   4 = Pinky

Guitar Fingerboard Chart

Frets 1–12

STRINGS

6th	5th	4th	3rd	2nd	1st
E	A	D	G	B	E

FRETS

STRINGS

Fret	6th	5th	4th	3rd	2nd	1st
Open	E	A	D	G	B	E
1st Fret	F	A#/B♭	D#/E♭	G#/A♭	C	F
2nd Fret	F#/G♭	B	E	A	C#/D♭	F#/G♭
3rd Fret	G	C	F	A#/B♭	D	G
4th Fret	G#/A♭	C#/D♭	F#/G♭	B	D#/E♭	G#/A♭
5th Fret	A	D	G	C	E	A
6th Fret	A#/B♭	D#/E♭	G#/A♭	C#/D♭	F	A#/B♭
7th Fret	B	E	A	D	F#/G♭	B
8th Fret	C	F	A#/B♭	D#/E♭	G	C
9th Fret	C#/D♭	F#/G♭	B	E	G#/A♭	C#/D♭
10th Fret	D	G	C	F	A	D
11th Fret	D#/E♭	G#/A♭	C#/D♭	F#/G♭	A#/B♭	D#/E♭
12th Fret	E	A	D	G	B	E

Fingerboard diagram

Strings (left to right): 6th 5th 4th 3rd 2nd 1st — E A D G B E

Fret	6th	5th	4th	3rd	2nd	1st
1st	F	A#/B♭	D#/E♭	G#/A♭	C	F
2nd	F#/G♭	B	E	A	C#/D♭	F#/G♭
3rd	G	C	F	A# / B♭	D	G
4th	G#/A♭	C#/D♭	F#/G♭	B	D#/E♭	G#/A♭
5th	A	D	G	C	E	A
6th	A#/B♭	D#/E♭	G#/A♭	C#/D♭	F	A#/B♭
7th	B	E	A	D	F# / G♭	B
8th	C	F	A#/B♭	D#/E♭	G	C
9th	C#/D♭	F#/G♭	B	E	G#/A♭	C#/D♭
10th	D	G	C	F	A	D
11th	D#/E♭	G#/A♭	C#/D♭	F#/G♭	A#/B♭	D#/E♭
12th	E	A	D	G	B	E